Fast Track to
JavaScript

From Zero to hero in 24 Hours

SUMAN DAS

This book is lovingly dedicated to my elder sisters —

Tandra Roy, Mandra Naskar, Chandra Mondal and Indra Khatua

whose unwavering support, guidance, and encouragement have been my greatest strength. Your love and wisdom have shaped my journey, and this book stands as a tribute to the inspiration you have given me

Contents

CONTENTS

Foreword

JavaScript is more than just a programming language—it's the foundation of the modern web, powering everything from interactive websites to advanced web applications. Whether you are a complete beginner or someone looking to sharpen your skills, this book, **"Fast Track to JavaScript - From Zero to Hero in 24 Hours,"** is designed to be your ultimate learning companion.

This book follows a **structured, hour-by-hour approach**, making JavaScript **easy to understand, accessible, and engaging** for beginners. **Even if you have never written a single line of code before, you can follow along and start building real-world applications step by step.**

What Makes This Book Special?

- ✓ **Beginner-Friendly Approach** – Written in **simple, easy-to-understand English** for readers with no prior coding experience.

- ✓ **Hands-On Learning** – Every chapter is filled with **real-world examples, code snippets, and practical exercises**.

- ✓ **Hour-Based Structure** – Learn at your own pace, one hour at a time, covering **everything from basics to advanced concepts like ES6+ features, asynchronous JavaScript, and APIs**.

- ✓ **Complete Assignment Solutions** – Unlike many books, this one provides **fully explained solutions for every assignment**, ensuring that you not only practice but also understand each concept deeply.

- ✓ **Covers ES6+ and Modern JavaScript** – Stay up-to-date with the **latest JavaScript features** and best practices.

Who Should Read This Book?

- • **Absolute Beginners** – If you have never coded before, this book will take you from **zero to hero**.

- **Students & Aspiring Developers** – Build a **strong foundation** in JavaScript for web development.

- **Self-Learners & Hobbyists** – A perfect guide for those who want to learn JavaScript **at their own pace**.

JavaScript is one of the most **powerful and in-demand** programming languages today, and mastering it opens up endless possibilities in web development. With this book as your guide, you will not only learn JavaScript but also develop the confidence to build real-world projects.

So, get ready to embark on your **JavaScript journey**—from **zero to hero in just 24 hours.**

Preface

JavaScript is the **language of the web**, powering everything from interactive websites to powerful web applications. Whether you are an absolute beginner with no prior programming experience or someone looking to strengthen your JavaScript fundamentals, this book, **"Fast Track to JavaScript – From Zero to Hero in 24 Hours,"** is your ultimate guide to mastering JavaScript **step by step, hour by hour**.

Why This Book?

Learning to code can be **intimidating**, especially for beginners. Most programming books assume some prior knowledge, leaving newcomers struggling with complex concepts. **This book takes a different approach**—it is written in **simple, easy-to-understand language**, with numerous examples, detailed explanations, and real-world use cases. Here's what makes this book unique:

- ✓ **Designed for complete beginners** – No prior coding experience needed.
- ✓ **Step-by-step learning** – Each hour builds upon the previous one.
- ✓ **Hands-on approach** – Every concept is explained with **clear examples and outputs**.
- ✓ **Real-world use cases** – Practical applications to understand why each concept matters.
- ✓ **Assignments with solutions** – Every hour includes **three practical exercises** with **detailed solutions**.
- ✓ **10 short answer-type questions per hour** – Helps reinforce learning and test understanding.
- ✓ **Latest JavaScript Features (ES6 and beyond)** – Learn modern JavaScript with **arrow functions, let and const, spread/rest operators, async/await, and more**.

Who Is This Book For?

This book is for **anyone** who wants to learn JavaScript quickly and effectively:

- ✓ **Absolute Beginners** – If you've never written a single line of code, don't worry! This book starts from scratch.

- ✓ **Students & Self-Learners** – If you're learning JavaScript for school, college, or personal projects, this book will be your best guide.
- ✓ **Aspiring Web Developers** – JavaScript is the foundation of web development. Master it to create dynamic websites and applications.
- ✓ **Programmers from Other Languages** – If you know Python, Java, or C++, this book will help you transition smoothly into JavaScript.

How This Book Is Structured

The book is divided into **24 Hours (Chapters)**, each covering a crucial topic in JavaScript. **Every hour follows a structured format:**

- ✓ **Concept Explanation** – Clear and beginner-friendly definitions.
- ✓ **Examples with Output** – Understand how JavaScript works in real scenarios.
- ✓ **Use Cases** – Learn how concepts apply in real-world applications.
- ✓ **Assignments** – Three practical exercises per hour, with detailed solutions.
- ✓ **10 Short Answer Questions** – Test your understanding with concise explanations.

Additionally, the book contains:

- ✔ **Appendix A: JavaScript Cheat Sheet** – A quick reference guide for key concepts and syntax.
- ✔ **Appendix B: Common JavaScript Errors & Fixes** – Troubleshoot mistakes like a pro.

Learning JavaScript **doesn't have to be difficult**. With the right approach, **you can master it in just 24 hours!**

I hope this book makes your **JavaScript learning journey smooth, enjoyable, and rewarding**. Let's start coding and turn you from a **beginner to a JavaScript hero!**

Suman Das

March 2025

Introduction

Why This Book?

JavaScript is the **backbone of the modern web**. Whether you want to create **interactive websites, build web applications, or dive into full-stack development**, JavaScript is the first step.

This book, **"Fast Track to JavaScript – From Zero to Hero in 24 Hours,"** is designed for **absolute beginners** who have never coded before. It takes you from **zero knowledge to confidently writing JavaScript programs in just 24 hours**.

What makes this book unique?

- ✓ **Step-by-step explanations** in **super easy English**.
- ✓ **Lots of examples** with **outputs** to make learning smooth.
- ✓ **Hands-on assignments** after every hour to test your skills.
- ✓ **Complete solutions** for all assignments, so you're never stuck.
- ✓ **Short answer questions** in each hour to reinforce key concepts.
- ✓ **Real-world use cases** to show how JavaScript is used practically.

Who Is This Book For?

This book is for:
- ✓ Absolute beginners who have **never programmed before**.
- ✓ Students and professionals who want to **learn JavaScript quickly**.
- ✓ Web designers who want to add **interactive features** to their websites.
- ✓ Programmers who know other languages but **want to master JavaScript**.

You **don't need any prior programming knowledge** to follow this book. By the end, you'll be comfortable writing JavaScript code and building interactive web applications.

How Is This Book Structured?

The book is divided into **24 hours**, where each hour covers a specific JavaScript topic.
- ✓ **Each hour includes:**
- ✓ **Easy-to-understand theory** with simple explanations.

- ✓ **Code examples** with **step-by-step breakdowns**.
- ✓ **Use cases** to show real-world applications.
- ✓ **Assignments** with **three practical exercises**.
- ✓ **Full solutions** to all assignments for **self-learning**.
- ✓ **10 short-answer questions** to test your knowledge.

The book also contains:
- ✓ **Appendices** for quick reference (JavaScript Cheat Sheet, Common Errors, and Additional Resources).
- ✓ **A structured learning path** that builds your skills from basics to advanced concepts.

What Will You Learn?

Here's a quick look at what you'll master in just **24 hours**:
- ✓ **JavaScript Basics** – Variables, Data Types, Operators
- ✓ **Control Flow** – If-else conditions, Loops
- ✓ **Functions & Objects** – Reusable code & Object-oriented concepts
- ✓ **DOM Manipulation** – Making web pages interactive
- ✓ **Events & Forms** – Handling user interactions
- ✓ **ES6+ Features** – Modern JavaScript (let, const, arrow functions, spread, destructuring)
- ✓ **Asynchronous JavaScript** – Callbacks, Promises, async/await
- ✓ **APIs & JSON** – Fetching and using real-world data
- ✓ **Error Handling & Debugging** – Fixing bugs like a pro
- ✓ **Project Development** – Applying JavaScript to real-world scenarios

By the end, you'll be **writing JavaScript code like a pro** and ready to dive into frameworks like **React, Node.js, or Vue.js**.

Why Learn JavaScript Now?

- ✓ JavaScript is the **most in-demand programming language** in the world. It powers **95% of all websites**, including Google, Facebook, and Amazon.
- ✓ **High demand for JavaScript developers** = Better job opportunities.
- ✓ **The core language of web development** – Essential for front-end, back-end, and full-stack development.
- ✓ **Beginner-friendly & versatile** – Learn once, use everywhere (web, mobile, and even AI).

This book is your **fast track to mastering JavaScript**. Whether you're a **student, professional, or hobbyist**, you'll gain **practical coding skills** in just 24 hours.

So, let's start this exciting journey and become a JavaScript Hero!

Fast Track
to
JavaScript

Hour 1
Introduction to JavaScript

Welcome to your journey into JavaScript! In this first hour, we will start from the absolute basics and understand what JavaScript is, why it is important, and how it works in a web page. We will also set up our development environment and write our very first JavaScript program. 

Evolution of JavaScript & Choosing the Right Version for Learning

❖ How JavaScript Was Created?

JavaScript was created in **1995** by **Brendan Eich** while working at **Netscape Communications Corporation**. Netscape wanted a scripting language for its web browser **Netscape Navigator** to make web pages interactive.

✓ Key Facts About JavaScript's Creation:

- Developed in **just 10 days** and was initially called **Mocha**.
- Renamed **LiveScript**, and then finally named **JavaScript** to capitalize on Java's popularity.
- Initially, it was only used for **client-side scripting** in browsers.
- Later, it evolved into a powerful language used for **server-side development (Node.js), mobile apps, and even AI/ML applications**.

JavaScript quickly became the **standard language** for the web, leading to the development of **ECMAScript (ES)** – a standard to ensure consistency across different implementations of JavaScript.

❖ Versions of JavaScript & ECMAScript Evolution

JavaScript follows **ECMAScript (ES)** standards. Below are the major ECMAScript versions and their key features:

[1]   ECMAScript 1 (ES1) – 1997

- The **first official standard** for JavaScript.
- Included basic features like **data types, loops, functions, and objects.**

[2]   ECMAScript 2 (ES2) – 1998

- Small updates to align with the **international standard (ISO/IEC 16262).**

[3]   **ECMAScript 3 (ES3) – 1999**

- Added **regular expressions**, try...catch for error handling, and better string handling.
- **Supported by all modern browsers.**

[4]   **ECMAScript 4 (ES4) – Canceled**

- This version was too ambitious and never officially released.

[5]   **ECMAScript 5 (ES5) – 2009 (Still widely used today)**

- **Strict Mode ("use strict")** to prevent common coding errors.
- Added **JSON support (JSON.parse(), JSON.stringify())**.
- Introduced **Array methods** like map(), filter(), forEach(), and reduce().
- **Backward compatible** with older JavaScript.

[6]   **ECMAScript 6 (ES6) – 2015 (Major Upgrade & Still the Most Important)**

- **Introduced let and const** (replacing var for better variable management).
- **Arrow functions (=>)** for shorter syntax.
- **Template literals (```)** for easier string formatting.
- **Destructuring ({} and [])** for extracting values from objects and arrays.
- **Spread (...) and Rest (...) operators** for handling multiple values easily.
- **Promises and async/await** for better asynchronous programming.
- **Default parameters** for functions.

[7]   **ECMAScript 7 (ES7) – 2016**

- Added Array.prototype.includes() method.
- **Exponentiation operator (**)** for math operations.

[8]   **ECMAScript 8 (ES8) – 2017**

- **Object.entries() and Object.values()** to work with objects more easily.
- **async/await improved** for better asynchronous coding.

[9]   **ECMAScript 9 (ES9) – 2018**

- **Rest/Spread properties for objects** ({ ...obj }).
- **Asynchronous iteration (for await...of)**.

[10]   ECMAScript 10 (ES10) – 2019

- **Array.prototype.flat()** to flatten nested arrays.
- **Object.fromEntries()** to convert key-value pairs into objects.

[11]   ECMAScript 11 (ES11) – 2020

- **Optional chaining (?.)** to safely access deeply nested properties.
- **Nullish coalescing operator (??)** for better default values.

[12]   ECMAScript 12 (ES12) – 2021

- **Logical assignment operators (&&=, ||=, ??=)**.
- **String replaceAll() method**.

[13]   ECMAScript 13 (ES13) – 2022

- **New at() method** for accessing array elements.
- **Top-level await** outside of async functions.

[14]   ECMAScript 14 (ES14) – 2023

- Improvements in **array and object handling**.
- **New regex match features**.

In this book, we are following **ES6 (2015) and newer versions**, as they offer modern features while maintaining compatibility with older versions.

❖ **Which JavaScript Version Are We Following in This Book?**

Why ES6+?

1. **Modern, cleaner syntax** (let, const, arrow functions).
2. **Better handling of asynchronous tasks** using **async/await**.
3. **Efficient object and array manipulation** (destructuring, spread/rest operators).
4. **More readable and maintainable code**.
5. **Better browser support** – Most modern browsers support ES6+ features.

However, ES5 is still relevant for older browsers, so we have covered ES5 concepts as well where necessary.

❖ **Is Learning JavaScript in 2025 Still Useful?**

Absolutely **YES!** JavaScript is one of the **most in-demand** and **versatile** programming languages today. **Why Learn JavaScript Now?**

✔ **JavaScript is Everywhere** – Web development, mobile apps, AI, game development, and even desktop applications.

✔ **Most Popular Programming Language** – JavaScript consistently ranks **#1 on Stack Overflow**.

✔ **Great for Beginners** – It has a **simple syntax** and can be run in any web browser without setup.

✔ **High Demand for JavaScript Developers** – React, Node.js, and front-end frameworks are booming.

✔ **The Future is JavaScript** – New frameworks and technologies (Next.js, Deno, and Bun) are built on JavaScript.

1.1 What is JavaScript?
1.1.1 Definition of JavaScript

JavaScript is a **programming language** that allows you to create **interactive** and **dynamic** content on websites. While **HTML** (HyperText Markup Language) structures a web page and **CSS** (Cascading Style Sheets) styles it, **JavaScript makes it interactive**.

✓ **Think of JavaScript as the brain of a webpage!**

1.1.2 Key Features of JavaScript

Feature	Description
Lightweight	JavaScript is easy to use and doesn't need heavy software installation.
Interpreted	It runs directly in the browser without needing compilation.
Dynamic	You can change web page content while the page is running.
Multi-platform	It works on different devices (PCs, mobile, tablets).
Event-driven	JavaScript reacts to user actions like clicks, typing, or scrolling.

1.1.3 Real-Life Example

You visit an e-commerce website and see a product list. When you click **"Add to Cart,"** the number of items in your cart updates immediately. That's JavaScript in action!

1.2 Why Learn JavaScript?

JavaScript is one of the most **popular** programming languages in the world. Let's explore why:

1.2.1 Why JavaScript is Important?

1. **JavaScript is Everywhere!**
   - It is used in **web development, mobile apps, game development, and even artificial intelligence (AI).**
2. **Easy to Learn**
   - JavaScript has a beginner-friendly syntax.
3. **Works with Other Technologies**
   - JavaScript works well with HTML and CSS to build websites.
4. **Great Career Opportunities**
   - Many companies look for JavaScript developers!

1.2.2 Use Case: Where is JavaScript Used?

Application Area	Example
Web Development	Adding animations, forms, and pop-ups to websites.
Mobile Apps	Frameworks like React Native help create mobile apps using JavaScript.
Game Development	Games like 2048 and Chrome Dino use JavaScript.
AI & Machine Learning	Libraries like TensorFlow.js allow JavaScript to be used for AI.

1.3 How JavaScript Works in a Web Page
1.3.1 Understanding the Role of JavaScript

A web page has three main parts:
1. **HTML** – Creates the structure (headings, buttons, paragraphs).
2. **CSS** – Styles the page (colors, fonts, layouts).
3. **JavaScript** – Makes the page interactive (buttons work, animations run).

   ✓ **Think of HTML as the skeleton, CSS as the skin, and JavaScript as the muscles that make the page move!**

1.3.2 How JavaScript Runs in the Browser?

Every modern browser (Chrome, Firefox, Edge) has a **JavaScript Engine** that executes JavaScript code.

1.3.3 Example: Simple HTML Page with JavaScript

```html
<!DOCTYPE html>
<html lang="en">
<head>
  <title>My First JavaScript</title>
</head>
<body>
  <h1>Welcome to JavaScript!</h1>
  <button onclick="showMessage()">Click Me</button>

  <script>
    function showMessage() {
      alert("Hello! You clicked the button.");
    }
  </script>
</body>
</html>
```

Output: When you click the button, a message box appears saying **"Hello! You clicked the button."**

1.4 Setting Up the Development Environment

To write and run JavaScript, you need:
1. **A Web Browser** – Chrome, Firefox, or Edge.
2. **A Code Editor** – VS Code (Visual Studio Code) is recommended.

1.4.1 Installing VS Code

1. Go to VS Code Website.
2. Download and install it.
3. Open VS Code and create a new file **(first.js or first.html).**

1.4.2 Using the Browser Console

Every browser has a **Developer Console** where you can run JavaScript.
1. Open Chrome.
2. Right-click → **Inspect** → **Go to Console Tab.**
3. Type: console.log("Hello, JavaScript!");
4. Press **Enter** and see the output.

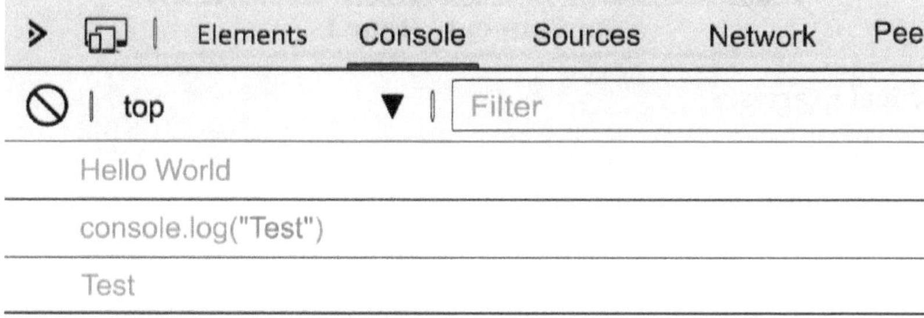

1.5 Writing Your First JavaScript Program

1.5.1 Printing a Message

```javascript
console.log("Hello, World!");
```

Output:

```
Hello, World!
```

1.5.2 Declaring Variables

```javascript
let name = "Alice";
console.log("Hello, " + name + "!");
```

Output:

```
Hello, Alice!
```

1.5.3 Simple Addition Program

```javascript
let num1 = 10;
let num2 = 20;
let sum = num1 + num2;
console.log("The sum is: " + sum);
```

Output:

```
The sum is: 30
```

Practical Exercises

1. Write a JavaScript program to display **"Welcome to JavaScript!"** in the browser console.
2. Write a program to add **two numbers** and print the result in the console.
3. Create an HTML page with a **button** that, when clicked, shows an alert message **"Button Clicked!"**

Short Answer Questions

1. What is JavaScript?
2. How does JavaScript make web pages interactive?
3. What are the three main components of a web page?
4. Name two web browsers that support JavaScript.
5. What is the role of the JavaScript console?
6. How do you display a message in the console?
7. What is the output of console.log("Hello, World!");?
8. Why is JavaScript called an interpreted language?
9. Name two places where JavaScript is used other than web development.
10. What is the difference between HTML, CSS, and JavaScript?

Congratulations! You have completed **Hour 1** and learned the basics of JavaScript. You now know **what JavaScript is, how it works in a web page, how to set up a development environment, and how to write your first JavaScript program.**

In **Hour 2**, we will explore **JavaScript Variables and Data Types** in detail!

Hour 2
JavaScript Basics

Welcome to **Hour 2** of your JavaScript journey! In this hour, we will cover the fundamental building blocks of JavaScript. You will learn about **variables, data types, comments, and console logging**—all essential skills for writing your first programs.

Everything will be explained **in very simple terms** with **plenty of examples** so that even someone with **zero programming experience** can understand.

2.1 Variables and Data Types
2.1.1 What Are Variables?

A **variable** is like a **container** that holds data. Imagine a **box** where you store information like numbers, words, or true/false values.

Why Do We Need Variables?

- To **store** information.
- To **reuse** values in our program.
- To **change** values when needed.

2.1.2 Declaring Variables in JavaScript

In JavaScript, we use **var, let, or const** to create variables.

Example: Declaring a Variable

```
var name = "John";
let age = 25;
const country = "India";
```

Explanation:

- var name = "John"; → Creates a variable name and stores "John".
- let age = 25; → Creates a variable age and stores 25.
- const country = "India"; → Creates a **constant** variable that **cannot be changed.**

2.1.3 Understanding var, let, and const

Keyword	Can Change Value?	Scope	Use Case
var	Yes	Function	Older method (avoid

Keyword	Can Change Value?	Scope	Use Case
		Scope	using)
let	Yes	Block Scope	Use for changeable variables
const	No	Block Scope	Use for fixed values

Example: Difference Between let and const

```
let x = 10;
x = 20; // Works fine

const y = 15;
y = 25; // Error! You can't change a const variable
```

2.2 Data Types in JavaScript

Data types define **what kind of data** we store in a variable. JavaScript has **six** main data types:

Data Type	Example	Description
String	"Hello"	Text data
Number	100, 5.75	Numeric values
Boolean	true, false	Yes/No values
Undefined	let x;	No value assigned
Null	let y = null;	Empty value
Object	{name: "Tom"}	Complex data

2.2.1 Strings

Strings store **text data** inside **quotes (" " or ' ')**.

Example: Working with Strings

```
let message = "Hello, World!";
console.log(message);
```

Output:

```
Hello, World!
```

String Properties and Methods

Method	Description	Example
.length	Finds length	"Hello".length → 5
.toUpperCase()	Converts to uppercase	"hello".toUpperCase() → "HELLO"
.toLowerCase()	Converts to lowercase	"HELLO".toLowerCase() → "hello"

2.2.2 Numbers

Numbers store **numeric data** (integers or decimals).

Example: Working with Numbers

```
let price = 99.99;
let quantity = 5;
let total = price * quantity;
console.log(total);
```

Output:

```
499.95
```

Common Number Methods

Method	Description	Example
.toFixed(2)	Rounds number	5.678.toFixed(2) → 5.68
.toString()	Converts to string	(123).toString() → "123"

2.2.3 Boolean Values

A **Boolean** stores only **true** or **false**.

Example: Boolean Usage

```
let isRaining = true;
let isSunny = false;
console.log(isRaining);
console.log(isSunny);
```

Output:

```
true
false
```

Boolean in Conditions

```
let age = 18;
let canVote = age >= 18;
console.log(canVote); // true
```

2.3 Comments and Code Readability
2.3.1 What Are Comments?

Comments are **ignored by JavaScript** but help explain your code.
Types of Comments:
- **Single-line comment (//)**
- **Multi-line comment (/* ... */)**

Example: Using Comments

```
// This is a single-line comment
let name = "Alice";


/*
  This is a multi-line comment
  It explains the following code
*/
let age = 30;
```

2.4 Console Logging and Debugging Basics
2.4.1 What is console.log()?

console.log() prints messages to the **browser console**.

Example: Printing to Console

```
console.log("JavaScript is fun!");
```

Output:

```
JavaScript is fun!
```

2.4.2 Using console.log() for Debugging

You can check values in your program using console.log().

Example: Debugging with Console

```
let a = 5;
let b = 10;
let sum = a + b;
console.log("The sum is:", sum);
```

Output:

```
The sum is: 15
```

Use Case: Simple Calculator

Let's use **variables, numbers, and console logging** to build a simple calculator!

Example: Addition Calculator

```
let num1 = 10;
let num2 = 20;
let sum = num1 + num2;
console.log("The sum of", num1, "and", num2, "is", sum);
```

Output:

```
The sum of 10 and 20 is 30
```

Exercise 1: Declare and Print Variables

Create a program that declares a let variable for your name, age, and country. Print them using console.log().

Exercise 2: Use String and Number Methods

Write a program that:
- Declares a number and rounds it to **2 decimal places**.
- Declares a string and converts it to **uppercase**.

Exercise 3: Boolean Logic

Create a program that checks if a person is **eligible to drive** (Age ≥ 18). Print true or false.

Short Answer Questions - Hour 2

1. What is a variable in JavaScript?
2. What are the three ways to declare a variable?
3. What is the difference between let and const?
4. What are the main data types in JavaScript?
5. How do you check the length of a string?
6. What is the purpose of console.log()?
7. How do you write a single-line comment in JavaScript?
8. What are Boolean values?
9. What is the difference between undefined and null?
10. How do you concatenate two strings in JavaScript?

In this hour, you learned **how to declare variables, use different data types, add comments, and print output to the console**. In the next hour, we will explore **operators and expressions** to perform calculations and make decisions. See you there!

Hour 3
Operators and Expressions

Understanding How JavaScript Performs Calculations and Evaluations

3.1 Introduction to Operators and Expressions

In JavaScript, an **operator** is a symbol that performs an operation on values or variables. These values are called **operands**. When operators and operands are combined, they form an **expression**.
For example:

```
let sum = 5 + 3; // Here, + is the operator, and 5 and 3 are operands.
console.log(sum); //
```

Output: 8

Operators are essential in programming because they help in performing calculations, comparisons, and logical evaluations.

3.2 Arithmetic Operators

Arithmetic operators are used to perform basic mathematical operations like addition, subtraction, multiplication, and division.

3.2.1 List of Arithmetic Operators in JavaScript

Operator	Symbol	Example	Explanation	Output
Addition	+	5 + 3	Adds two numbers	8
Subtraction	-	10 - 4	Subtracts second number from first	6
Multiplication	*	6 * 2	Multiplies two numbers	12
Division	/	9 / 3	Divides first number by second	3
Modulus	%	10 % 3	Returns remainder of division	1
Exponentiation	**	2 ** 3	Raises first number to the power of second	8

3.2.2 Examples of Arithmetic Operators
Example 1: Performing Basic Calculations

```
let a = 10;
let b = 5;

console.log(a + b);  // Output: 15
console.log(a - b);  // Output: 5
console.log(a * b);  // Output: 50
console.log(a / b);  // Output: 2
console.log(a % b);  // Output: 0
console.log(a ** b); // Output: 100000
```

Example 2: Using Arithmetic Operators in a Real-World Scenario

Imagine you are a store owner and need to calculate the total cost of items a customer buys.

```
let pricePerItem = 50;
let quantity = 3;
let totalCost = pricePerItem * quantity;

console.log("Total cost of items: $" + totalCost); //
```

Output: Total cost of items: $150

3.3 Comparison Operators

Comparison operators compare two values and return either true or false.

3.3.1 List of Comparison Operators

Operator	Symbol	Example	Explanation	Output
Equal to	==	5 == '5'	Checks if values are equal (ignores type)	true
Strict Equal	===	5 === '5'	Checks if values and types are equal	false
Not Equal	!=	10 != 5	Checks if values are not equal	true
Strict Not Equal	!==	10 !== '10'	Checks if values and types are not equal	true
Greater Than	>	8 > 5	Checks if first value is greater	true
Less Than	<	3 < 7	Checks if first value is smaller	true

Operator	Symbol	Example	Explanation	Output
Greater or Equal	>=	5 >= 5	Checks if first value is greater or equal	true
Less or Equal	<=	2 <= 4	Checks if first value is smaller or equal	true

3.3.2 Examples of Comparison Operators

Example 1: Checking Age Eligibility

```
let age = 18;
console.log(age >= 18); //
```

Output: true

Example 2: Checking Password Match

```
let password = "abc123";
let userInput = "abc123";

console.log(password === userInput); //
```

Output: true

3.4 Logical Operators

Logical operators are used to perform logical operations and return true or false.

3.4.1 List of Logical Operators

Operator	Symbol	Example	Explanation	Output
AND	&&	true && false	Returns true if both are true	false
OR	`		`	`true
NOT	!	!true	Returns the opposite value	false

3.4.2 Examples of Logical Operators

Example 1: Checking Login Credentials

```
let username = "admin";
let password = "12345";

console.log(username === "admin" && password === "12345"); //
```

Output: true

Example 2: Checking Discount Eligibility

```
let isMember = true;
let hasCoupon = false;

console.log(isMember || hasCoupon); //
```

Output: true

3.5 String Concatenation and Template Literals
3.5.1 Concatenation Using + Operator

```
let firstName = "John";
let lastName = "Doe";
let fullName = firstName + " " + lastName;
console.log(fullName); //
```

Output: John Doe

3.5.2 Using Template Literals (Backticks `)

```
let name = "Alice";
let age = 25;
console.log(`Hello, my name is ${name} and I am ${age} years old.`);
```

Output: Hello, my name is Alice and I am 25 years old.

3.6 Operator Precedence

Operator precedence determines which operations are performed first.

3.6.1 Operator Precedence Table

Precedence	Operator	Description
1	( )	Parentheses
2	**	Exponentiation
3	*, /, %	Multiplication, Division, Modulus
4	+, -	Addition, Subtraction
5	>, <, >=, <=	Comparison Operators
6	&&, `	

3.6.2 Example of Operator Precedence

```
console.log(2 + 3 * 4);  //
```

Output: 14 (Multiplication first)

```
console.log((2 + 3) * 4); //
```

Output: 20 (Parentheses first)

Practical Exercises

1. Write a program that takes two numbers and prints their sum, difference, product, and quotient.
2. Create a JavaScript program that checks whether a user is eligible for a senior citizen discount (age 60 or above).
3. Write a program that asks the user for a number and checks if it is even or odd.

Short Answer Questions

1. What is an operator in JavaScript?
2. What is the difference between == and ===?
3. What does the modulus operator % do?
4. What are logical operators?
5. How do you concatenate strings in JavaScript?
6. What is the purpose of parentheses in operator precedence?
7. Give an example of a program that uses comparison operators.
8. What will be the output of 5 + "5"?
9. How do template literals differ from normal string concatenation?
10. What is the difference between && and ||?

This completes **Hour 3: Operators and Expressions**. Let me know if you want modifications before we proceed to **Hour 4**!

Introduction

In real life, we make decisions all the time. For example, if it's raining, we take an umbrella. If we are hungry, we eat food. Similarly, in programming, we use **conditional statements** to make decisions based on conditions.

Conditional statements allow the program to make decisions based on certain conditions. Think of it like a traffic light system:

- If the light is **green**, you **go**.
- If the light is **red**, you **stop**.
- If the light is **yellow**, you **slow down**.

Similarly, in programming, we use **conditional statements** to control what happens next based on different conditions.

JavaScript provides **if-else statements, switch cases, and truthy/falsy values** to control the flow of the program. These allow our programs to make choices and perform different actions based on different situations.

Let's explore these in detail!

4.1 If-Else Statements

The **if-else** statement is one of the most important concepts in programming. It helps a program **make decisions** based on whether a condition is **true** or **false**.

4.1.1 Syntax of If-Else Statement

Here's the basic structure of an if-else statement:

```
if (condition) {
    // Code to run if condition is true
} else {
    // Code to run if condition is false
}
```

4.1.2 Example 1: Checking Age for Voting Eligibility

Let's write a simple program to check if a person is eligible to vote.

```
let age = 18;

if (age >= 18) {
    console.log("You are eligible to vote.");
```

```
} else {
    console.log("You are not eligible to vote.");
}
```

Output:

```
You are eligible to vote.
```
If age is **less than 18**, the output would be:
```
You are not eligible to vote.
```

4.1.3 Example 2: Checking Even or Odd Numbers

```
let number = 7;

if (number % 2 === 0) {
    console.log("The number is even.");
} else {
    console.log("The number is odd.");
}
```

Output:

```
The number is odd.
```

4.1.4 If-Else Use Case
Scenario: Imagine a bank where customers need a minimum balance of $500 to withdraw money.

```
let balance = 400;

if (balance >= 500) {
    console.log("You can withdraw money.");
} else {
    console.log("Insufficient balance. Deposit more money.");
}
```

Output:

```
Insufficient balance. Deposit more money.
```
This shows how if-else statements help make real-world decisions in programming.

4.2 Nested If-Else Statements

A nested if-else statement is when you place an if-else inside another if-else.

4.2.1 Example of Nested If-Else

Let's check if a student has passed based on marks.

```
let marks = 85;

if (marks >= 50) {
  if (marks >= 80) {
    console.log("You passed with distinction!");
  } else {
    console.log("You passed!");
  }
} else {
  console.log("You failed.");
}
```

Output

```
You passed with distinction!
```

4.2.2 Use Case

Scenario: Checking if a user is eligible for a discount.

```
let isMember = true;
let totalPurchase = 100;

if (isMember) {
  if (totalPurchase >= 50) {
    console.log("You get a 20% discount!");
  } else {
    console.log("You get a 10% discount.");
  }
} else {
  console.log("No discount available.");
}
```

Output:

```
'You get a 20% discount!'
```

4.3 Else-If Ladder

Sometimes, we need to check multiple conditions. In such cases, we use an **else-if ladder**.

4.3.1 Syntax of Else-If Ladder

```
if (condition1) {
    // Code to run if condition1 is true
} else if (condition2) {
    // Code to run if condition2 is true
} else {
    // Code to run if none of the conditions are true
}
```

4.3.2 Example: Grading System

Let's write a program that assigns grades based on marks.

```
let marks = 85;

if (marks >= 90) {
    console.log("Grade: A");
} else if (marks >= 80) {
    console.log("Grade: B");
} else if (marks >= 70) {
    console.log("Grade: C");
} else {
    console.log("Grade: F");
}
```

Output:

```
Grade: B
```

4.4 Switch Case Statement

When there are multiple options, a **switch case** is more readable than multiple if-else statements.

4.4.1 Syntax of Switch Case

```
switch(expression) {
  case value1:
    // Code to run if expression === value1
    break;
  case value2:
    // Code to run if expression === value2
    break;
  default:
    // Code to run if no case matches
```

```
}
```

4.4.2 Example: Day of the Week

Let's write a program that prints the name of the day based on a number (1-7).

```javascript
let day = 3;

switch (day) {
  case 1:
    console.log("Monday");
    break;
  case 2:
    console.log("Tuesday");
    break;
  case 3:
    console.log("Wednesday");
    break;
  case 4:
    console.log("Thursday");
    break;
  case 5:
    console.log("Friday");
    break;
  case 6:
    console.log("Saturday");
    break;
  case 7:
    console.log("Sunday");
    break;
  default:
    console.log("Invalid day number");
}
```

Output:

```
Wednesday
```

4.4.3 Use Case

Scenario: A vending machine that dispenses drinks based on selection.

```javascript
let choice = "Coke";
```

```javascript
switch (choice) {
  case "Coke":
    console.log("You selected Coke.");
    break;
  case "Pepsi":
    console.log("You selected Pepsi.");
    break;
  case "Water":
    console.log("You selected Water.");
    break;
  default:
    console.log("Invalid selection.");
}
```

4.5 Truthy and Falsy Values

In JavaScript, some values are **truthy** (treated as true) and some are **falsy** (treated as false) when used in conditions.

4.5.1 Falsy Values

The following values are considered **falsy**:

Falsy Value	Description
false	Boolean false
0	The number zero
"" (empty string)	A string with no characters
null	Represents an empty or unknown value
undefined	A variable that has not been assigned a value
NaN	Not a Number

4.5.2 Truthy Values

Anything that is **not falsy** is considered **truthy**. Some examples:

```javascript
if ("Hello") {
  console.log("This is truthy!");
}

if (100) {
  console.log("This is also truthy!");
}
```

Output:

```
This is truthy!
This is also truthy!
```

Type	Truthy Values	Falsy Values
Numbers	Any number except 0	0
Strings	Any non-empty string	"" (empty string)
Objects/Arrays	Any object or array	null, undefined
Boolean	true	false

4.5.3 Example of Truthy and Falsy Values

```javascript
let name = "John";

if (name) {
   console.log("Name is provided.");
} else {
   console.log("No name given.");
}
```

Output

```
Name is provided.
If name was an empty string (""), the output would be:
No name given.
```

4.5.4 Use Case

Scenario: Checking if a user provided input in a form.

```javascript
let userInput = "";

if (userInput) {
   console.log("Thank you for providing input.");
} else {
   console.log("Input is required.");
}
```

4.6 Use Cases of Conditional Statements
Example 1: Checking User Login Status

```javascript
let isLoggedIn = true;

if (isLoggedIn) {
   console.log("Welcome back, user!");
```

```
} else {
    console.log("Please log in.");
}
```

Output:

```
Welcome back, user!
```

Example 2: Online Store Discounts

```
let customerType = "Premium";

if (customerType === "Premium") {
    console.log("You get a 20% discount!");
} else if (customerType === "Regular") {
    console.log("You get a 10% discount!");
} else {
    console.log("No discount available.");
}
```

Output:

```
You get a 20% discount!
```

Exercise 1: Temperature Checker

Write a JavaScript program that checks the temperature and prints:
- "It's too cold!" if temperature < 10
- "It's warm." if temperature is between 10 and 25
- "It's hot!" if temperature > 25

Exercise 2: Leap Year Checker

Write a program to check if a given year is a **leap year** or not.

Exercise 3: Password Strength Checker

Write a JavaScript program that checks if a password length is:
- "Weak" if less than 6 characters
- "Medium" if between 6 and 10 characters
- "Strong" if more than 10 characters

Short Answer Questions

1. What is an if-else statement?
2. What is the difference between if-else and switch case?
3. What happens if no case matches in a switch statement?
4. Name three falsy values in JavaScript.
5. What is a truthy value?
6. Why do we use break statements in switch cases?
7. Write an example of an if-else statement.
8. What is the purpose of an else-if ladder?
9. How does JavaScript handle empty strings in conditions?
10. What will be the output of the following code?

```
if (0) {
  console.log("Truthy");
} else {
  console.log("Falsy");
}
```

This completes **Hour 4**! These concepts will help you make smart decisions in programming.

Hour 5
Loops and Iterations

Mastering Repetitive Tasks in JavaScript

5.1 Introduction to Loops

In programming, we often need to repeat certain actions multiple times. For example, imagine you are creating a website and want to display numbers from 1 to 10. Instead of writing 10 separate console.log() statements, we can use **loops** to automate this process.

A **loop** is a programming structure that **repeats a block of code** as long as a specified condition is met.

JavaScript provides **three main types of loops**:

1. for loop – Best when you know how many times you want to repeat an action.
2. while loop – Used when we want to repeat an action **until** a certain condition is met.
3. do-while loop – Similar to while but ensures the loop runs **at least once** before checking the condition.

5.2 The for Loop
5.2.1 Understanding the for Loop

A for loop is used when we know **how many times** we need to repeat a task.

Syntax of a for Loop:

```
for (initialization; condition; update) {
   // Code to execute
}
```

- **Initialization**: Sets a starting value (e.g., let i = 1).
- **Condition**: Specifies how long the loop should run (e.g., i <= 10).
- **Update**: Changes the loop variable after each iteration (e.g., i++ increases i by 1).

5.2.2 Example: Counting from 1 to 5

```
for (let i = 1; i <= 5; i++) {
   console.log("Number:", i);
}
```

Output:

```
Number: 1
Number: 2
Number: 3
Number: 4
Number: 5
```

5.2.3 Example: Printing Even Numbers from 2 to 10

```javascript
for (let i = 2; i <= 10; i += 2) {
   console.log(i);
}
```

Output:

```
2
4
6
8
10
```

5.2.4 Use Case: Displaying a List of Products

Loops are useful in real-world applications like displaying product names dynamically.

```javascript
let products = ["Laptop", "Phone", "Tablet"];

for (let i = 0; i < products.length; i++)
{
   console.log("Product:", products[i]);
}
```

Output:

```
Product: Laptop
Product: Phone
Product: Tablet
```

5.3 The while Loop
5.3.1 Understanding the while Loop

A while loop runs **as long as the condition is true**.

Syntax:

```javascript
while (condition) {
   // Code to execute
}
```

5.3.2 Example: Counting from 1 to 5

```
let i = 1;
while (i <= 5) {
   console.log("Number:", i);
   i++;
}
```

Output:

```
Number: 1
Number: 2
Number: 3
Number: 4
Number: 5
```

5.3.3 Use Case: Checking a Password Until It Matches

Imagine a login system where a user must enter the correct password.

```
let correctPassword = "hello123";
let userInput = "";

while (userInput !== correctPassword) {
   userInput = prompt("Enter password: ");
}
console.log("Access granted!");
```

This loop runs **until** the user enters "hello123".

5.4 The do-while Loop
5.4.1 Understanding the do-while Loop

A do-while loop ensures the code inside **runs at least once**, even if the condition is false.

Syntax:

```
do {
   // Code to execute
} while (condition);
```

5.4.2 Example: Asking for User Input

```
let number;
do {
   number = prompt("Enter a number greater than 10:");
} while (number <= 10);
```

```
console.log("You entered:", number);
```

This ensures the user enters a valid number **at least once**.

5.5 Breaking and Continuing Loops
5.5.1 break Statement (Stopping a Loop Early)

The break statement **exits a loop immediately** when a condition is met.
Example: Stop the loop when i reaches 3.

```
for (let i = 1; i <= 5; i++) {
  if (i === 3) {
    break;
  }
  console.log(i);
}
```

Output:

```
1
2
```

5.5.2 continue Statement (Skipping an Iteration)

The continue statement **skips** the current loop iteration and moves to the next one.
Example: Skip printing number 3.

```
for (let i = 1; i <= 5; i++) {
  if (i === 3) {
    continue;
  }
  console.log(i);
}
```

Output:

```
1
2
4
5
```

5.6 Using Loops with Arrays and Strings
5.6.1 Looping Through an Array

```
let fruits = ["Apple", "Banana", "Cherry"];
for (let i = 0; i < fruits.length; i++) {
```

```
    console.log(fruits[i]);
}
```

Output:

```
Apple
Banana
Cherry
```

5.6.2 Looping Through a String

```
let word = "HELLO";
for (let i = 0; i < word.length; i++) {
    console.log(word[i]);
}
```

Output:

```
H
E
L
L
O
```

5.7 Extra Properties of Loops (Table Format)

Feature	for Loop	while Loop	do-while Loop
Use Case	When the number of iterations is known	When the number of iterations is unknown	Ensures at least one execution
Condition Check	Before each iteration	Before each iteration	After the first execution
Best Used For	Counting, Iterating Arrays	Waiting for User Input, Checking Conditions	Ensuring a Task Runs at Least Once

Exercise 1: Print Multiplication Table

Write a program to print the multiplication table of 5 using a for loop.

Exercise 2: Sum of Numbers Until User Enters 0

Write a while loop that asks the user to enter numbers and keeps adding them until the user enters 0. Display the sum.

Exercise 3: Reverse a String Using a Loop

Write a JavaScript program to reverse a string using a loop.

Short Answer Questions – Hour 5

1. What is a loop in JavaScript?
2. How does a for loop work?
3. What are the three parts of a for loop?
4. How does a while loop differ from a for loop?
5. What is the main advantage of a do-while loop?
6. What does the break statement do?
7. What does the continue statement do?
8. How can you loop through an array using a for loop?
9. How do you use a loop to print characters of a string one by one?
10. Give a real-world example where loops are useful.

This structured chapter will help a **complete beginner** master loops with **clear explanations, examples, use cases, and exercises**. Let me know if you need any changes!

Hour 6
Functions and Scope

JavaScript functions are an essential part of programming, allowing us to write reusable and structured code. In this hour, we will learn:

1. What functions are and why they are important
2. How to define and call functions
3. How to pass values to functions and return results
4. The difference between function declarations and expressions
5. Understanding **scope** (Global and Local variables)

By the end of this hour, you will be able to write your own functions, make your code more organized, and understand how JavaScript handles variables within different parts of a program.

6.1 What is a Function?

A **function** is a block of code designed to perform a specific task. Instead of writing the same code multiple times, we can **define a function once** and **call it whenever needed**.

Why Use Functions?

- **Reusability**: Write once, use multiple times.
- **Better Code Organization**: Helps in structuring code efficiently.
- **Easier Debugging**: If something goes wrong, we only need to check the function instead of the whole program.

Example of a Function

```
function greet() {
    console.log("Hello, Welcome to JavaScript!");
}
greet(); // Calling the function
```

Output:

```
Hello, Welcome to JavaScript!
```

6.2 Defining and Calling Functions

A function in JavaScript is defined using the **function** keyword followed by a **name** and a pair of parentheses ().

6.2.1 Syntax of a Function

```
function functionName() {
```

```
  // Code to execute
}
```

To **use** a function, we need to **call it** by writing its name followed by ().

Example: Function to Display a Message

```
function sayHello() {
   console.log("Hello, how are you?");
}
sayHello(); // Function call
```

Output:

```
Hello, how are you?
```

6.3 Function Parameters and Return Values
6.3.1 Function Parameters

Functions can take **input values** called **parameters**. These values are passed inside the parentheses () when calling the function.

Example: Function with Parameters

```
function greetUser(name) {
   console.log("Hello, " + name + "!");
}
greetUser("John");
greetUser("Alice");
```

Output:

```
Hello, John!
Hello, Alice!
```

6.3.2 Returning Values from Functions

Sometimes, we want a function to process some data and **return a value** instead of just printing it.

Example: Function Returning a Value

```
function addNumbers(a, b) {
   return a + b;
}

let sum = addNumbers(5, 10);
console.log("The sum is: " + sum);
```

Output:

```
The sum is: 15
```

6.4 Function Expressions vs Function Declarations
6.4.1 Function Declaration

A **function declaration** defines a function using the function keyword.

```
function multiply(a, b) {
   return a * b;
}


console.log(multiply(4, 3)); // Output: 12
```

6.4.2 Function Expression

A **function expression** stores a function inside a variable.

```
let multiply = function(a, b) {
   return a * b;
};


console.log(multiply(4, 3)); // Output: 12
```

Key Differences

Feature	Function Declaration	Function Expression
Hoisting	Can be called before defining	Cannot be called before defining
Naming	Has a function name	Usually stored in a variable
Usage	More common for defining reusable functions	Used for anonymous functions and callbacks

6.5 Understanding Scope (Global vs Local Variables)
Scope determines where variables are accessible in a program.
6.5.1 Global Scope
A **global variable** is declared **outside any function** and can be accessed anywhere in the script.

```
let globalVar = "I am global";

function showGlobal() {
   console.log(globalVar);
```

```
}

showGlobal(); // Output: I am global
```

6.5.2 Local Scope

A **local variable** is declared **inside a function** and can only be used within that function.

```
function showLocal() {
  let localVar = "I am local";
  console.log(localVar);
}


showLocal(); // Output: I am local
console.log(localVar); // Error: localVar is not defined
```

6.5.3 Block Scope (let & const)

With let and const, variables are **only accessible inside the block {}** where they are declared.

```
{
  let blockVar = "Inside block";
  console.log(blockVar); // Works
}
console.log(blockVar); // Error: blockVar is not defined
```

Use Case Example: Managing Shopping Cart Total

```
let cartTotal = 0; // Global variable

function addToCart(price) {
  cartTotal += price;
}

addToCart(20);
addToCart(30);
console.log("Total price: $" + cartTotal); // Output: Total price: $50
```

Practical Exercises

1. Write a function that takes a number as input and returns its square.
2. Create a function that checks if a given number is even or odd.
3. Write a function that takes two numbers and returns the larger of the two.

Short Answer Questions

1. What is a function in JavaScript?
2. How do you define and call a function?
3. What are function parameters?
4. What does the return statement do in a function?
5. Explain the difference between function declaration and function expression.
6. What is a global variable?
7. What is a local variable?
8. What is the difference between var, let, and const in terms of scope?
9. What is function hoisting?
10. Write an example of a function that returns a string.

This concludes **Hour 6**! In the next hour, we will dive deeper into **objects and arrays**, learning how to structure data efficiently in JavaScript.

Hour 7
JavaScript Objects and Arrays

In this hour, we will explore two of the most important data structures in JavaScript: **Objects and Arrays**. These structures help store, organize, and manipulate data efficiently.

By the end of this hour, you will learn:

- What objects and arrays are
- How to create and access object properties
- How to work with arrays
- Common array methods with practical examples

7.1 Understanding Objects (Key-Value Pairs)
7.1.1 What is an Object?

In JavaScript, an **object** is a collection of **key-value pairs**. It helps store multiple values under a single variable, making data more structured.

Example of an Object:

```
let person = {
  name: "John",
  age: 25,
  city: "New York"
};
console.log(person);
```

Output:

```
{ name: 'John', age: 25, city: 'New York' }
```

Here,

- name, age, and city are **keys**.
- "John", 25, and "New York" are **values**.

7.1.2 Creating an Object

You can create an object in two ways:

1. Using Object Literal (Recommended)

```
let car = {
  brand: "Toyota",
  model: "Camry",
  year: 2023
```

```
};
console.log(car);
```

2. Using the new Object() Syntax

```
let car = new Object();
car.brand = "Toyota";
car.model = "Camry";
car.year = 2023;


console.log(car);
```

Both methods create an object that stores information about a car.

7.2 Creating and Accessing Object Properties
7.2.1 Accessing Object Properties

You can access values in an object using **dot notation** or **bracket notation**.

1. Dot Notation (Recommended)

```
console.log(person.name); // Output: John
```

2. Bracket Notation

```
console.log(person["age"]); // Output: 25
```

Bracket notation is useful when keys are dynamic or contain spaces.

7.2.2 Modifying Object Properties

Objects are **mutable**, meaning you can modify their values.

```
person.city = "Los Angeles";
console.log(person.city); // Output: Los Angeles
```

7.2.3 Adding and Deleting Properties

You can add a new property or remove an existing one.

Adding a Property

```
person.country = "USA";
console.log(person);
```

Deleting a Property

```
delete person.age;
console.log(person);
```

7.3 Array Basics: Creating, Accessing, and Modifying
7.3.1 What is an Array?

An **array** is a collection of values stored in a single variable. Arrays are **ordered**, meaning each value has an **index** (starting from 0).

Example of an Array:

```
let fruits = ["Apple", "Banana", "Orange"];
console.log(fruits);
```

Output:

```
["Apple", "Banana", "Orange"]
```

7.3.2 Creating an Array

You can create an array in two ways:

1. Using Square Brackets (Recommended)

```
let numbers = [10, 20, 30, 40, 50];
```

2. Using the new Array() Syntax

```
let numbers = new Array(10, 20, 30, 40, 50);
```

7.3.3 Accessing Array Elements

Each element in an array has an **index**, starting from **0**.

```
console.log(fruits[0]); // Output: Apple
console.log(fruits[1]); // Output: Banana
```

7.3.4 Modifying an Array

```
fruits[1] = "Mango";
console.log(fruits); // Output: ["Apple", "Mango", "Orange"]
```

7.4 Array Methods (push, pop, shift, unshift, slice, splice)
7.4.1 Adding and Removing Elements

Method	Description	Example	Output
push()	Adds an element at the end	fruits.push("Grapes")	["Apple", "Mango", "Orange", "Grapes"]
pop()	Removes the last element	fruits.pop()	["Apple", "Mango"]

Method	Description	Example	Output
unshift()	Adds an element at the beginning	fruits.unshift("Strawberry")	["Strawberry", "Apple", "Mango", "Orange"]
shift()	Removes the first element	fruits.shift()	["Apple", "Mango", "Orange"]

7.4.2 Extracting and Replacing Elements

Extracting a Portion (slice())

```
let someFruits = fruits.slice(1, 3);
console.log(someFruits); // Output: ["Mango", "Orange"]
```

slice(start, end) method is used to extract a portion of an array **without modifying the original array**. It returns a **new array** containing the selected elements.

Understanding slice(1, 3)

```
let fruits = ["Apple", "Mango", "Orange", "2", "3"];
let someFruits = fruits.slice(1, 3);
console.log(someFruits);
```

Step-by-Step Execution
Array Indexing in JavaScript:

Apple → **Index 0**
Mango → **Index 1**
Orange → **Index 2**
"2" → **Index 3**
"3" → **Index 4**

Understanding slice(1, 3)

1 → **Start index** (Inclusive) → Starts from "Mango".
3 → **End index** (Exclusive) → Stops **before** "2" (index 3).
So, slice(1, 3) extracts elements from index **1** (Mango) **up to, but not including** index **3** (which is "2").

Output of console.log(someFruits);

```
["Mango", "Orange"]
```

slice(start, end) extracts elements from **start index (inclusive)** to **end index (exclusive)**. The **original array remains unchanged**.

slice(1, 3) returns **["Mango", "Orange"]**.

Understanding slice() with Negative Indexes

In JavaScript, the slice() method also accepts negative indexes, which count elements from the end of the array instead of the beginning.
Example with Negative Indexes

```
let fruits = ["Apple", "Mango", "Orange", "2", "3"];
let someFruits = fruits.slice(-3, -1);
console.log(someFruits);
```

Step-by-Step Execution
Negative Indexing in JavaScript:

"Apple" → Index -5
"Mango" → Index -4
"Orange" → Index -3
"2" → Index -2
"3" → Index -1

Understanding slice(-3, -1)

-3 → Start index (inclusive) → Starts from "Orange".
-1 → End index (exclusive) → Stops before "3" (index -1).
So, slice(-3, -1) extracts elements from index -3 (Orange) up to, but not
including index -1 (which is "3").
Output of console.log(someFruits);
["Orange", "2"]

Comparison of Positive and Negative Indexing

Expression	Extracted Elements	Explanation
slice(1, 3)	["Mango", "Orange"]	Starts from index 1 and stops before 3
slice(-3, -1)	["Orange", "2"]	Starts from third last element and stops before last element

✓ Negative indexes count from the end of the array.

✓ The second parameter is always exclusive (not included in the result).

✓ The original array remains unchanged.

Adding/Removing Elements (splice())

```
fruits.splice(1, 1, "Peach");
console.log(fruits); // Output: ["Apple", "Peach", "Orange"]
```

Understanding splice(1, 1, "Peach") in JavaScript

In JavaScript, the splice() method is used to **add, remove, or replace elements in an array**. Unlike slice(), which **does not modify** the original array, splice() **modifies** the original array.

Syntax of splice()

```
array.splice(start, deleteCount, item1, item2, ...);
```

- start → **Index where changes begin**.
- deleteCount → **Number of elements to remove**.
- item1, item2, ... → **Elements to insert** at the start index.

Example

```
let fruits = ["Apple", "Mango", "Orange"];
fruits.splice(1, 1, "Peach");
console.log(fruits);
```

Step-by-Step Execution

1. **Initial Array:**
2. ["Apple", "Mango", "Orange"]
3. **Understanding splice(1, 1, "Peach")**
   - 1 → **Start index (1st position, i.e., "Mango")**.
   - 1 → **Deletes 1 element ("Mango")**.
   - "Peach" → **Inserted at index 1** (replacing "Mango").
4. **Final Array after Modification:**
5. ["Apple", "Peach", "Orange"]

```
["Apple", "Peach", "Orange"]
```

How splice() Works in Different Cases

Expression	Effect	Output
fruits.splice(1, 1, "Peach")	Replaces "Mango" with "Peach"	["Apple", "Peach", "Orange"]
fruits.splice(1, 0, "Peach")	Inserts "Peach" at index 1 (without deleting anything)	["Apple", "Peach", "Mango", "Orange"]

Expression	Effect	Output
fruits.splice(1, 2, "Peach")	Replaces "Mango" and "Orange" with "Peach"	["Apple", "Peach"]
fruits.splice(2, 1)	Deletes "Orange" without adding anything	["Apple", "Mango"]

✓ splice() **modifies** the original array.

✓ It can **remove, replace, or insert** elements at any position.

✓ The **second parameter (deleteCount) is crucial**—if 0, nothing is removed.

Use Case: Organizing Student Records with Objects and Arrays

Imagine you are storing student records. You can use objects and arrays together.

```
let students = [
   { name: "Alice", age: 20, course: "JavaScript" },
   { name: "Bob", age: 22, course: "Python" }
];

console.log(students[0].name); // Output: Alice
console.log(students[1].course); // Output: Python
```

Assignment - Hour 7

1. Create an Object

- Create an object book with properties: title, author, yearPublished.
- Access and print author using both dot and bracket notation.

2. Modify an Array

- Create an array colors with three color names.
- Add two colors at the end and remove the first one.
- Print the final array.

3. Use Object and Array Together

- Create an array movies with objects inside. Each object should have title, year, and rating.
- Print the name of the first movie.

Short Answer Questions (Hour 7)

1. What is an object in JavaScript?
2. How do you access an object's property using dot notation?
3. How do you add a new property to an object?
4. What is the difference between an object and an array?
5. What does the push() method do in an array?
6. How do you remove the first element from an array?
7. What does slice() do in an array?
8. How do you replace an element in an array?
9. How do you store multiple student records using objects and arrays?
10. Explain the use of splice() in arrays.

This lesson ensures that even a **complete beginner** can understand and use **objects and arrays** effectively in JavaScript.

Hour 8
Advanced Array Methods

Arrays are one of the most important concepts in JavaScript. In this hour, we will learn about advanced array methods like forEach, map, filter, and reduce. These methods help us work with arrays efficiently by performing actions like iterating over elements, transforming data, filtering specific values, and reducing an array into a single value. We will also learn how to sort and search within arrays.

By the end of this hour, you will be comfortable handling complex operations on arrays using simple, powerful JavaScript methods.

8.1 Understanding Advanced Array Methods

Before diving into specific methods, let's understand **why we need them**.
Imagine you have a list of numbers and you want to:

- Perform an operation on every number (like doubling each value).
- Filter out certain numbers (like getting only even numbers).
- Add up all the numbers to find the total sum.
- Transform the list into something new (like converting numbers to strings).

Doing this with traditional for loops can be time-consuming and make the code complex. Instead, JavaScript provides **higher-order functions** (functions that operate on other functions) to make these tasks easier.
Let's explore them one by one.

8.2 forEach() – Looping Through an Array
8.2.1 What is forEach()?

The forEach() method is used to loop through an array and execute a function for each element. It does not return anything (undefined).
8.2.2 Syntax
```
array.forEach(function(element, index, array) {
   // Code to execute for each element
});
```
- element → The current value in the array.
- index (optional) → The index of the current element.
- array (optional) → The original array.

8.2.3 Example: Print Each Element

```
let numbers = [10, 20, 30, 40];
```

```
numbers.forEach(function(num) {
  console.log(num);
});
```

Output:

```
10
20
30
40
```

8.2.4 Example: Print Elements with Index

```
let fruits = ["Apple", "Banana", "Cherry"];

fruits.forEach(function(fruit, index)
 {
   console.log(`Index ${index}: ${fruit}`);
});
```

Output:

```
Index 0: Apple
Index 1: Banana
Index 2: Cherry
```

8.2.5 Use Case: Updating Prices in an E-Commerce Store

Suppose we need to **increase all product prices by 10%**.

```
let prices = [100, 200, 300];

prices.forEach(function(price, index, arr) {
   arr[index] = price + (price * 0.10);  // Increase price by 10%
});

console.log(prices);
```

Output:

```
[110, 220, 330]
```

8.3 map() – Transforming an Array
8.3.1 What is map()?

The map() method **creates a new array** by applying a function to each element. Unlike forEach(), it returns a transformed array.

8.3.2 Syntax

```
let newArray = array.map(function(element, index, array) {
  return element * 2;
});
```

8.3.3 Example: Double Each Number

```
let numbers = [2, 4, 6, 8];

let doubled = numbers.map(function(num) {
  return num * 2;
});

console.log(doubled);
```

Output:

```
[4, 8, 12, 16]
```

8.3.4 Example: Convert Prices from Dollars to Rupees

```
let pricesInDollars = [10, 20, 30];

let pricesInRupees = pricesInDollars.map(function(price) {
  return price * 82;  // Assume $1 = ₹82
});

console.log(pricesInRupees);
```

Output:

```
[820, 1640, 2460]
```

8.4 filter() – Extracting Specific Data
8.4.1 What is filter()?

The filter() method **returns a new array** with elements that pass a given condition.

8.4.2 Example: Filter Even Numbers

```javascript
let numbers = [1, 2, 3, 4, 5, 6];
let evens = numbers.filter(function(num) {
    return num % 2 === 0;
});
console.log(evens);
```

Output:

```
[2, 4, 6]
```

8.4.3 Example: Filter Out Adults (Age >= 18)

```javascript
let ages = [12, 18, 25, 15, 30];

let adults = ages.filter(function(age) {
    return age >= 18;
});

console.log(adults);
```

Output:

```
[18, 25, 30]
```

8.5 reduce() – Calculating a Single Value
8.5.1 What is reduce()?

The reduce() method **reduces an array** to a single value (like sum or product).

8.5.2 Syntax

```javascript
let result = array.reduce(function(accumulator, element) {
    return accumulator + element;
}, initialValue);
```

8.5.3 Example: Sum of All Numbers

```javascript
let numbers = [10, 20, 30, 40];

let total = numbers.reduce(function(sum, num) {
    return sum + num;
}, 0);

console.log(total);
```

Output:

```
100
```

8.6 Sorting and Searching in Arrays
8.6.1 Sorting (sort())

Sorting and searching are essential operations when working with arrays in JavaScript. Sorting helps arrange data in order, while searching allows us to find specific elements efficiently.

Sorting in JavaScript (sort())

The sort() method sorts the elements of an array **alphabetically** by default. However, when sorting numbers, we need to provide a comparison function.

Example 1: Sorting an Array of Strings (Alphabetical Order)

```javascript
let fruits = ["Banana", "Apple", "Mango", "Cherry"];
fruits.sort();
console.log(fruits);
```

Output:

```
["Apple", "Banana", "Cherry", "Mango"]
```

Example 2: Sorting an Array of Numbers (Ascending Order)

By default, sort() sorts numbers as strings, so 100 comes before 2. To fix this, we use a comparison function.

```javascript
let numbers = [100, 2, 45, 10, 1];
numbers.sort((a, b) => a - b);
console.log(numbers);
```

Output:

```
[1, 2, 10, 45, 100]
```

Example 3:

```javascript
let numbers = [40, 10, 30, 20];

numbers.sort();
console.log(numbers);
```

Output:

```
[10, 20, 30, 40]
```

8.6.2 Searching in JavaScript (indexOf(), find(), and filter())

Searching helps find the index or value of an element in an array.

Example 4: Searching for an Element Using indexOf()

The indexOf() method returns the **index** of an element in an array. If the element is not found, it returns -1.

```
let colors = ["Red", "Blue", "Green", "Yellow"];
let index = colors.indexOf("Green");
console.log(index);
```

Output:

```
2
```

Example 5: Finding an Element Using find()

The find() method returns **the first element** that matches a condition.

```
let numbers = [10, 25, 8, 99, 55];
let result = numbers.find(num => num > 20);
console.log(result);
```

Output:

```
25  // The first number greater than 20
```

Example 5: Filtering Elements Using filter()

The filter() method returns **all elements** that match a condition.

```
let numbers = [10, 25, 8, 99, 55];
let filteredNumbers = numbers.filter(num => num > 20);
console.log(filteredNumbers);
```

Output:

```
[25, 99, 55]  // All numbers greater than 20
```

Practical Exercises

1. Write a program that multiplies all numbers in an array by 5 using map().
2. Write a program that filters out all numbers greater than 50 from an array.
3. Create an array of prices and use reduce() to calculate the total bill.

8.8 Short Answer Questions

1. What does the forEach() method do?
2. How does map() differ from forEach()?
3. What is the use of filter() in arrays?
4. How do you find the sum of numbers in an array using reduce()?
5. What does the sort() method do?
6. Can map() modify the original array?
7. What are the parameters of forEach()?
8. How can you filter out odd numbers from an array?
9. What will be the output of ["z", "b", "a"].sort()?
10. What is the initial value in reduce() used for?

This completes **Hour 8**, covering advanced array methods in **easy, beginner-friendly language** with **many examples.**

Hour 9
Working with Strings

Welcome to **Hour 9** of learning JavaScript! In this hour, we will focus on **strings**—a fundamental data type used to store and manipulate text in JavaScript.

By the end of this hour, you will understand:

- How strings work in JavaScript.
- Different methods to manipulate strings.
- The basics of **regular expressions**.
- String **interpolation** using template literals.

Each section will include **simple explanations, multiple examples, and outputs** to ensure that even a complete beginner can grasp the concepts easily.

9.1 What is a String?

A **string** is a sequence of characters enclosed in **single quotes (' ')**, **double quotes (" ")**, or **backticks ( )**.

9.1.1 Declaring a String

In JavaScript, you can declare a string in three ways:

```
let string1 = "Hello, World!";  // Using double quotes
let string2 = 'JavaScript is fun!';  // Using single quotes
let string3 = `I am learning JavaScript!`; // Using backticks
```

All three methods work the same way, but backticks have additional features, which we will explore later.

9.2 Common String Methods

JavaScript provides **many built-in methods** to manipulate strings. Let's explore the most commonly used ones.

9.2.1 Finding the Length of a String (length Property)

The **length** property tells us how many characters are in a string.

Example:

```
let message = "Hello, JavaScript!";
console.log(message.length);
```

Output:

```
18
```

The length includes **spaces and punctuation** as well.

9.2.2 Extracting Parts of a String (slice())

The **slice(start, end)** method extracts a part of a string. The **start index is included, but the end index is not**.

Example:

```
let text = "JavaScript Programming";
let part = text.slice(0, 10);
console.log(part);
```

Output:

```
JavaScript
```

If the end index is omitted, it slices till the end of the string.

```
console.log(text.slice(11));
```

Output:

```
Programming
```

9.2.3 Splitting a String into an Array (split())

The **split(separator)** method breaks a string into an array based on a specified separator.

Example:

```
let sentence = "Learning JavaScript is fun";
let words = sentence.split(" ");  // Splitting by space
console.log(words);
```

Output:

```
["Learning", "JavaScript", "is", "fun"]
```

9.2.4 Replacing Part of a String (replace())

The **replace(oldValue, newValue)** method replaces text in a string.

Example:

```
let text = "I love Python";
let newText = text.replace("Python", "JavaScript");
```

```
console.log(newText);
```

Output:

```
I love JavaScript
```

Only the **first match** is replaced.

9.2.5 Converting to Uppercase and Lowercase

- toUpperCase() – Converts to **uppercase**.
- toLowerCase() – Converts to **lowercase**.

Example:

```
let word = "JavaScript";
console.log(word.toUpperCase()); // "JAVASCRIPT"
console.log(word.toLowerCase()); // "javascript"
```

9.2.6 Trimming Spaces (trim())

The **trim()** method removes spaces from **both ends** of a string.

Example:

```
let message = "   Hello, World!   ";
console.log(message.trim());
```

Output:

```
"Hello, World!"
```

9.3 Regular Expressions Basics

Regular expressions (**RegEx**) help search for patterns in strings.

Example: Checking if a String Contains a Word

```
let sentence = "JavaScript is amazing!";
let check = /JavaScript/.test(sentence);
console.log(check);
```

Output:

```
true
```

The **test()** method checks if a pattern exists in the string.

9.4 String Interpolation and Template Literals

Backticks (` `) allow **string interpolation**, making it easier to insert variables into strings.

Example:

```
let name = "Alice";
let age = 25;
console.log(`My name is ${name} and I am ${age} years old.`);
```

Output:

```
My name is Alice and I am 25 years old.
```

Template literals also support **multi-line strings**.

Example:

```
let message = `This is line 1
This is line 2
This is line 3`;
console.log(message);
```

Output:

```
This is line 1
This is line 2
This is line 3
```

9.5 Summary Table of String Methods

Method	Description	Example	Output
length	Returns string length	"Hello".length	5
slice(start, end)	Extracts part of a string	"JavaScript".slice(0,4)	"Java"
split(separator)	Splits a string into an array	"a,b,c".split(",")	["a", "b", "c"]
replace(old, new)	Replaces text in a string	"abc".replace("a", "z")	"zbc"
toUpperCase()	Converts to uppercase	"abc".toUpperCase()	"ABC"
toLowerCase()	Converts to lowercase	"ABC".toLowerCase()	"abc"
trim()	Removes spaces from both ends	" Hello ".trim()	"Hello"

Practical Exercises

1. Write a JavaScript program that asks for a user's full name and prints:
   - The name in **uppercase**.
   - The name in **lowercase**.
   - The **length** of the name.
2. Create a function that takes a **sentence** and returns an **array** of words.
3. Write a program that **replaces** the word "bad" with "good" in a given sentence.

Short Answer Questions

1. What is a string in JavaScript?
2. How do you find the length of a string?
3. What is the difference between slice() and split()?
4. How does replace() work in JavaScript?
5. What does trim() do?
6. What are template literals?
7. How do you convert a string to uppercase?
8. What is a regular expression?
9. What is string interpolation?
10. How can you remove extra spaces from a string?

This concludes **Hour 9** of your JavaScript journey! Now, practice these concepts before moving to the next hour.

Hour 10
Understanding the DOM
(Document Object Model)

JS

10.1 What is the DOM?

10.1.1 Understanding the DOM in Simple Terms

Imagine a web page as a **tree-like structure**, where each part of the webpage (headings, paragraphs, images, buttons) is a branch. This structure is called the **Document Object Model (DOM).**

In simple words, the **DOM** is a way for JavaScript to interact with and change web pages dynamically. When a webpage loads, the browser creates a **model of the page** that JavaScript can use to access and modify elements like text, images, or colors.

10.1.2 Why is the DOM Important?

- ☑ With JavaScript and the DOM, you can:
  Change text, colors, images, and styles dynamically
- ☑ Add or remove elements from a webpage
- ☑ Handle user interactions like clicks, typing, and mouse movements

10.1.3 Real-World Example of the DOM

Think about a **light switch**. If a webpage is a room, the light switch is JavaScript using the DOM. You can turn the light (color, text, elements) on and off by controlling the switch (JavaScript code).

10.1.4 How Browsers Create the DOM

When you open a webpage, the browser performs the following steps:

[1] Reads the **HTML code** and creates a **DOM tree.**
[2] Reads the **CSS code** and applies styles to the **DOM elements.**
[3] Runs the **JavaScript code**, which can change the **DOM structure** dynamically.

10.1.5 Example of a Simple Webpage and Its DOM
HTML Code:

```html
<!DOCTYPE html>
<html>
<head>
  <title>My First DOM Example</title>
</head>
```

```
<body>
  <h1 id="heading">Hello, World!</h1>
</body>
</html>
```

When the browser loads this page, it creates the following **DOM structure**:
Document

```
| — html
|   | — head
|   |          └───── title: "My First DOM Example"
|   | — body
|              └───── h1: "Hello, World!"
|
```

With JavaScript, we can **change** this heading dynamically, which we will learn next!

10.2 Selecting Elements in JavaScript
10.2.1 Methods to Select Elements

To manipulate the webpage using JavaScript, we first need to **select** the elements we want to change. JavaScript provides several methods to do this:

Method	Description
document.getElementById(id)	Selects an element using its ID
document.querySelector(selector)	Selects the first element that matches a CSS selector
document.querySelectorAll(selector)	Selects all elements that match a CSS selector

10.2.2 Selecting an Element by ID (getElementById)

☑ The **getElementById** method selects an element using its **ID**. **Best used when selecting a unique element.**

Example: Selecting and Changing a Heading

```
<!DOCTYPE html>
<html>
<head>
  <title>Change Text Example</title>
</head>
<body>
  <h1 id="myTitle">Original Title</h1>
  <button onclick="changeTitle()">Click Me</button>
```

```
  <script>
    function changeTitle() {
      let heading = document.getElementById("myTitle");
      heading.innerHTML = "New Title Updated!";
    }
  </script>
</body>
</html>
```

Output (Before Clicking the Button)
 ✦ Original Title
Output (After Clicking the Button)
 ✦ New Title Updated!

10.2.3 Selecting Elements with querySelector and querySelectorAll

☑   Best used for selecting elements using CSS selectors (class, tag, etc.).

Example: Selecting a Paragraph with querySelector

```
<p class="info">This is a paragraph.</p>
<script>
  let paragraph = document.querySelector(".info");
  paragraph.style.color = "blue";
</script>
```

Output:

The text color of the paragraph turns **blue**.

10.3 Modifying HTML and CSS with JavaScript
10.3.1 Changing Content with innerHTML

The **innerHTML** property allows us to **change** the content inside an HTML element.

Example: Changing Text Dynamically

```
<h2 id="demo">Welcome!</h2>
<button onclick="changeText()">Change</button>

<script>
  function changeText() {
    document.getElementById("demo").innerHTML = "Hello,
JavaScript!";
```

```
    }
</script>
```

Output:

Clicking the button changes "Welcome!" to **"Hello, JavaScript!"**.

10.3.2 Changing CSS Styles

We can modify **CSS properties** directly using **JavaScript**.

Example: Changing Background Color

```html
<p id="myPara">Click to change color</p>
<button onclick="changeColor()">Change Color</button>
<script>
  function changeColor() {
     document.getElementById("myPara").style.backgroundColor =
"yellow";
  }
</script>
```

Output:

The paragraph background turns **yellow** after clicking the button.

10.3.3 Adding and Removing Elements

We can **add** or **remove** elements dynamically using JavaScript.

Example: Adding a New Paragraph

```html
<button onclick="addPara()">Add Paragraph</button>
<div id="container"></div>

<script>
  function addPara() {
     let newPara = document.createElement("p");
     newPara.innerHTML = "This is a new paragraph!";
     document.getElementById("container").appendChild(newPara);
  }
</script>
```

Output:

Clicking the button **adds a new paragraph**.

1. **Create a webpage** where clicking a button **changes the font size** of a paragraph.
2. **Make a simple webpage** where clicking a button **adds a new list item** in an existing list.
3. **Create a page** where clicking a button **toggles the visibility** of an image.

Short Answer Questions - Hour 10

1. What is the DOM in JavaScript?
2. How does JavaScript interact with the DOM?
3. What does document.getElementById() do?
4. How is querySelector different from getElementById?
5. What property is used to change an element's text?
6. How can you change the background color of an element?
7. How do you add a new element to the DOM using JavaScript?
8. What is innerHTML used for?
9. How do you remove an element from the DOM?
10. What happens if an element with the given ID does not exist?

This hour ensures **absolute beginners** understand how JavaScript interacts with webpages using the **DOM**.

Hour 11
Event Handling in JavaScript

Making Web Pages Interactive with Events

Introduction to Event Handling

Web pages become interactive through **events**. An event occurs when a user does something, such as clicking a button, pressing a key, or moving the mouse. JavaScript allows us to detect these events and execute code in response. This is called **event handling**.

For example, when you click a "Submit" button, JavaScript can check whether you have filled out a form correctly. If not, it can show a warning message.

11.1 Adding Event Listeners

To handle events in JavaScript, we use **event listeners**. These are functions that wait for an event to happen and execute code when the event occurs.

11.1.1 The addEventListener() Method

The best way to add an event to an element is by using the addEventListener() method.

Syntax

```
element.addEventListener("event", function);
```

- element: The HTML element that listens for the event.
- event: The type of event (e.g., "click", "mouseover", "keydown").
- function: The function to execute when the event occurs.

11.1.2 Handling Click Events

A **click event** occurs when a user clicks on an element, such as a button.

Example: Changing Text on Click

```
<button id="myButton">Click Me</button>
<p id="output">Original Text</p>
<script>
  document.getElementById("myButton").addEventListener("click",
function() {
    document.getElementById("output").innerText = "You clicked the
button!";
```

```
  });
</script>
```


Output:

```
Before clicking: Original Text
After clicking: You clicked the button!
```

11.1.3 Handling Mouseover Events

A **mouseover event** occurs when the mouse pointer moves over an element.

Example: Changing Background Color on Mouseover

```
<div id="box" style="width: 200px; height: 100px; background-color:
lightgray;">
  Hover over me!
</div>

<script>
  document.getElementById("box").addEventListener("mouseover",
function() {
    this.style.backgroundColor = "yellow";
  });

  document.getElementById("box").addEventListener("mouseout",
function() {
    this.style.backgroundColor = "lightgray";
  });
</script>
```

Output:

When the user hovers over the box, the background turns
yellow.
When the user moves the mouse away, it turns **light gray** again.

11.1.4 Handling Keydown Events

A **keydown event** occurs when a user presses a key.

Example: Displaying the Pressed Key

```
<input type="text" id="textBox" placeholder="Type something">
<p id="keyOutput"></p>
```

```
<script>
  document.getElementById("textBox").addEventListener("keydown",
function(event) {
    document.getElementById("keyOutput").innerText = "You pressed: "
+ event.key;
  });
</script>
```

Output:

```
If you press the "A" key, it will display:
"You pressed: A"
```

11.2 Understanding the Event Object

Every event in JavaScript contains useful information about what happened. This information is stored in the **event object**.

Example: Using the Event Object

```
<button id="infoButton">Click for Info</button>
<p id="infoOutput"></p>

<script>
  document.getElementById("infoButton").addEventListener("click",
function(event) {
    document.getElementById("infoOutput").innerText =
    "Button clicked at X: " + event.clientX + ", Y: " + event.clientY;
  });
</script>
```

Output:

```
If you click at position (50, 100), it will show:
"Button clicked at X: 50, Y: 100"
```

11.3 Event Delegation

Event delegation allows us to handle events efficiently, especially when dealing with multiple elements. Instead of adding event listeners to each individual element, we add one listener to a parent element.

Example: Handling Clicks on Multiple Buttons

```
<div id="buttonContainer">
  <button class="childBtn">Button 1</button>
```

```html
  <button class="childBtn">Button 2</button>
  <button class="childBtn">Button 3</button>
</div>
<p id="result"></p>

<script>

document.getElementById("buttonContainer").addEventListener("clic
k", function(event) {
  if (event.target.classList.contains("childBtn")) {
    document.getElementById("result").innerText = "You clicked: " +
event.target.innerText;
  }
 });
</script>
```

Output:

```
If you click Button 2, it will show:
"You clicked: Button 2"
```

11.4 Form Validation with Events

JavaScript helps ensure users enter valid data in a form.

Example: Validating an Email Field

```html
<input type="email" id="emailInput" placeholder="Enter your email">
<button id="submitButton">Submit</button>
<p id="errorMessage" style="color: red;"></p>

<script>

document.getElementById("submitButton").addEventListener("click",
function() {
  let email = document.getElementById("emailInput").value;
  if (!email.includes("@")) {
    document.getElementById("errorMessage").innerText = "Please
enter a valid email!";
  } else {
    document.getElementById("errorMessage").innerText = "";
    alert("Form submitted successfully!");
  }
 });
```

```
</script>
```

Output:

If you enter "test.com", it will show "Please enter a valid email!"
If you enter "test@example.com", the form submits successfully.

Extra Properties Table

Property	Description
event.target	The element that triggered the event
event.type	The type of event (e.g., "click", "mouseover")
event.clientX	X-coordinate of the mouse click
event.clientY	Y-coordinate of the mouse click
event.key	The key that was pressed (for keyboard events)

Practical Exercises

1. Create a button that, when clicked, changes the background color of the entire page.
2. Make a text box that displays a **live word count** as the user types.
3. Build a simple **To-Do List** where clicking on a task removes it from the list.

Short Answer Questions

1. What is an event in JavaScript?
2. How do you attach an event listener to a button?
3. What is the purpose of addEventListener()?
4. Explain what happens in a **mouseover event**.
5. How does JavaScript detect **keypress events**?
6. What is the event object?
7. Why do we use event delegation?
8. What property gives the element that triggered an event?
9. How can JavaScript prevent a form from submitting if an input is incorrect?
10. Write the JavaScript code to detect when a user right-clicks on a webpage.

This **Hour 11** covers **everything about event handling** with **detailed explanations, examples, assignments, and quizzes**.

Hour 12
JavaScript Timing Functions

Mastering setTimeout(), setInterval(), and Animation Techniques

12.1 Introduction to JavaScript Timing Functions

Timing functions in JavaScript allow you to **schedule code execution** after a certain time or at repeated intervals. These functions are essential for:

- **Creating delays** in script execution.
- **Running repeated tasks**, such as updating a clock.
- **Animating elements** smoothly over time.

JavaScript provides two main timing functions:

1. setTimeout() – Runs a function **once** after a specified delay.
2. setInterval() – Runs a function **repeatedly** at a specified interval.

We will also learn how to **stop timers** and **animate elements** using these functions.

12.2 setTimeout(): Executing Code After a Delay

The setTimeout() function is used to **execute a function once** after a specified time.

12.2.1 Syntax of setTimeout()

setTimeout(function, delay);

- function → The function to be executed.
- delay → The time (in milliseconds) to wait before executing the function. (1 second = 1000 milliseconds)

12.2.2 Example: Displaying a Message After 3 Seconds

```
setTimeout(function() {
    console.log("Hello! This message appears after 3 seconds.");
}, 3000);
```

Output (After 3 seconds):

```
Hello! This message appears after 3 seconds.
```

12.2.3 Example: Changing Text After a Delay

```
function changeText() {
    document.getElementById("message").innerText = "Text changed
after 5 seconds!";
```

```
}
setTimeout(changeText, 5000);
```

HTML:

```
<p id="message">Wait for it...</p>
```

Use Case:
- Displaying **welcome messages** after a delay on a webpage.
- Showing **notifications** to users after some time.

12.3 setInterval(): Repeating Code at Intervals

The setInterval() function runs a function **repeatedly** at a specified interval.

12.3.1 Syntax of setInterval()

```
setInterval(function, interval);
```

- function → The function to execute.
- interval → The time (in milliseconds) between executions.

12.3.2 Example: Printing a Message Every 2 Seconds

```
setInterval(function() {
  console.log("This message appears every 2 seconds!");
}, 2000);
```

Output (Every 2 seconds):

```
This message appears every 2 seconds!
```

12.3.3 Example: Creating a Digital Clock

```
function showTime() {
  let now = new Date();
  document.getElementById("clock").innerText =
now.toLocaleTimeString();
}

setInterval(showTime, 1000);
```

HTML:

```
<p id="clock"></p>
```

Use Case:
- **Displaying a real-time clock** on a website.
- **Auto-updating stock prices** every few seconds.

12.4 Clearing Timers: clearTimeout() and clearInterval()

Timers should be stopped when no longer needed to **improve performance**.

12.4.1 Stopping a setTimeout() Execution

Use clearTimeout(timeoutVariable) to cancel a setTimeout().

Example: Canceling a Scheduled Message

```
let timeoutId = setTimeout(function() {
    console.log("This will not be printed.");
}, 5000);


clearTimeout(timeoutId); // Cancels the scheduled function
```

12.4.2 Stopping a setInterval() Execution

Use clearInterval(intervalVariable) to stop a repeating function.

Example: Stopping an Updating Counter

```
let count = 0;
let intervalId = setInterval(function() {
    count++;
    console.log(count);
    if (count === 5) clearInterval(intervalId); // Stops after 5 times
}, 1000);
```

Output:

```
1
2
3
4
5
```

12.5 Animating Elements with Timers

JavaScript timing functions can create animations by changing **CSS properties** over time.

12.5.1 Example: Moving a Box Across the Screen

```
let position = 0;
function moveBox() {
```

```
    position += 5;
    document.getElementById("box").style.left = position + "px";
    if (position < 300) setTimeout(moveBox, 50);
}

moveBox();
```

HTML & CSS:

```
<div id="box"></div>
<style>
  #box { width: 50px; height: 50px; background: red; position:
absolute; left: 0; }
</style>
```

Use Case:
- Creating **smooth animations** without heavy libraries.
- Moving elements **dynamically** on a webpage.

12.6 JavaScript Timing Functions Summary

Function	Description	Example Usage
setTimeout()	Executes code **once** after a delay.	setTimeout(myFunction, 3000);
setInterval()	Repeats code execution **at fixed intervals**.	setInterval(myFunction, 2000);
clearTimeout()	Cancels a **setTimeout()** before execution.	clearTimeout(timeoutId);
clearInterval()	Stops a **setInterval()** loop.	clearInterval(intervalId);

Exercise 1: Countdown Timer

Create a countdown timer that starts from 10 and decreases every second until it reaches 0.

Exercise 2: Blinking Text

Make a text blink every 500ms using setInterval().

Exercise 3: Stop a Timer

Create a button that starts a timer and another button that stops it.

12.8 Short Answer Questions

1. What is setTimeout() used for?
2. How does setInterval() work?
3. What is the difference between setTimeout() and setInterval()?
4. How can you stop a running setTimeout()?
5. How can you stop an ongoing setInterval()?
6. What unit is used for specifying delay in setTimeout()?
7. Write an example of setTimeout() that changes text after 2 seconds.
8. What is the use of clearInterval()?
9. How can JavaScript timing functions be used for animations?
10. Give one practical use case for setInterval().

This explanation ensures **even complete beginners** understand timing functions with **simple examples, practical use cases, and hands-on exercises**.

Would you like any modifications before moving to the next hour?

13.1 Introduction to Error Handling

JavaScript, like any programming language, sometimes runs into problems while executing code. These problems are called **errors**. If we do not handle them properly, they can cause our program to stop working. Error handling helps us manage these issues smoothly without crashing the entire program.

For example, imagine you are using a website, and suddenly it shows a **"Page Unresponsive"** message. That happens when errors are not handled properly. Good error handling ensures that even if something goes wrong, the rest of the website continues to function.

Types of Errors in JavaScript

JavaScript errors can be divided into three main types:

Error Type	Description	Example
Syntax Error	Happens when JavaScript code is not written correctly.	console.log("Hello) (Missing closing quote)
Reference Error	Occurs when trying to use a variable that does not exist.	console.log(myVariable); (if myVariable is not defined)
Type Error	Occurs when performing an invalid operation on a data type.	"Hello" - 5; (Subtracting a number from a string)

Now, let's explore how JavaScript helps us handle errors using try, catch, and finally.

13.2 Try, Catch, and Finally Blocks

The try...catch...finally statement is the most common way to handle errors in JavaScript.

- **try block** → Code that may cause an error is placed inside try.
- **catch block** → If an error occurs, JavaScript moves to catch and runs the code inside it.
- **finally block** → Runs code regardless of whether an error occurs or not.

Example 1: Handling an Error with try...catch

```
try {
    let a = 10;
    let b = a / 0; // Division by zero (valid in JS but logically incorrect)
    console.log("Result:", b);
} catch (error) {
    console.log("An error occurred:", error.message);
}
```

Output:

```
Result: Infinity
```

*In JavaScript, dividing by zero does not cause an error but returns **Infinity**. If it were another type of error (like using an undefined variable), the catch block would handle it.*

Example 2: Catching an Undefined Variable Error

```
try {
    console.log(myVariable); // myVariable is not defined
} catch (error) {
    console.log("Oops! An error occurred:", error.message);
}
```

Output:

```
Oops! An error occurred: myVariable is not defined
```

13.3 Handling Errors Gracefully

Good error handling ensures that users do not see ugly error messages. Instead, they get helpful feedback.

Example 3: Handling Input Errors

```
function divideNumbers(a, b) {
    try {
        if (typeof a !== "number" || typeof b !== "number") {
            throw new Error("Both inputs must be numbers");
        }
        if (b === 0) {
            throw new Error("Cannot divide by zero");
        }
        return a / b;
    } catch (error) {
```

```
    return "Error: " + error.message;
  }
}

console.log(divideNumbers(10, 2)); // Output: 5
console.log(divideNumbers(10, "two")); // Output: Error: Both inputs
must be numbers
console.log(divideNumbers(10, 0)); // Output: Error: Cannot divide by
zero
```

Explanation:

- We **manually throw an error** if the inputs are not numbers.
- If division by zero is attempted, an error is shown.
- The program does not crash and instead returns helpful messages.

13.4 Debugging with Browser DevTools

Debugging is the process of finding and fixing errors in the code. JavaScript provides tools inside the web browser to help with debugging.

How to Use the JavaScript Debugger

1. Open your **browser's Developer Tools** (Press **F12** or **Ctrl + Shift + I** in Chrome).
2. Go to the **Console** tab to see errors and logs.
3. Use **console.log()** to print values and debug your code.
4. Use **debugger;** to pause the script execution.

Example 4: Using console.log() for Debugging

```
let price = 100;
let discount = 20;
console.log("Original Price:", price);
console.log("Discount Applied:", discount);
console.log("Final Price:", price - discount);
```

Output in Console:

```
Original Price: 100
Discount Applied: 20
Final Price: 80
```

Example 5: Using the Debugger Statement

```
let num1 = 5;
let num2 = 10;
```

```
debugger; // The browser will pause execution here

let result = num1 + num2;
console.log("Result is:", result);
```

How it Works:

- The browser pauses execution when it hits debugger;, allowing you to inspect variables.

Use Case: Handling Errors in a Login System

Imagine you are building a login form. Users enter their email and password, but they might make mistakes.

Example: Validating Login Credentials

```
function loginUser(email, password) {
  try {
    if (!email.includes("@")) {
      throw new Error("Invalid email format");
    }
    if (password.length < 6) {
      throw new Error("Password must be at least 6 characters");
    }
    return "Login Successful!";
  } catch (error) {
    return "Login Failed: " + error.message;
  }
}

console.log(loginUser("userexample.com", "pass123")); // Invalid
email format
console.log(loginUser("user@example.com", "123")); // Password too
short
console.log(loginUser("user@example.com", "password123")); //
Login Successful!
```

Practical Exercises

1. Write a function that takes two numbers and divides them. If the second number is 0, throw an error saying **"Division by zero is not allowed"**.
2. Create a simple **calculator program** using try...catch. It should accept two numbers and an operation (+, -, *, /). Handle cases where the user enters an invalid number or an invalid operation.
3. Use **debugger;** in a function that calculates the sum of an array of numbers. Run it in the browser's DevTools to inspect variables.

Short Answer Questions

1. What is error handling in JavaScript?
2. Name three types of JavaScript errors.
3. What does the try block do?
4. How does the catch block work?
5. What is the purpose of the finally block?
6. What happens if an error is not caught using try...catch?
7. How do you manually throw an error in JavaScript?
8. What is the purpose of console.log() in debugging?
9. How can you pause JavaScript execution using the browser's debugger?
10. Give an example of an error message when trying to use an undefined variable.

This concludes **Hour 13: Error Handling and Debugging**!

Hour 14
JavaScript ES6+ Features

In this hour, we will explore some powerful features introduced in ES6 (ECMAScript 2015) and later versions. These features make JavaScript easier to write, understand, and maintain. Even if you have never coded before, don't worry! We will explain everything step by step with **simple definitions, examples, outputs, and real-world use cases.**

14.1 let and const vs var

Before ES6, JavaScript only had **var** for declaring variables. But ES6 introduced **let** and **const**, which are better and safer to use. Let's see how they work.

14.1.1 Understanding var, let, and const

1. var (Old Way)
- **Variables declared with var can be redeclared and reassigned.**
- **They are function-scoped, meaning they only exist inside the function where they were declared.**
- **They are hoisted (moved to the top) but not initialized.**

Example: Using var

```
var name = "John";
console.log(name); // Output: John

var name = "Alice"; // Redeclaration allowed
console.log(name); // Output: Alice
```

2. let (New and Safer Way)
- **Variables declared with let can be reassigned but not redeclared in the same scope.**
- **They are block-scoped, meaning they exist only inside {} where they were declared.**
- **They are hoisted but not initialized.**

Example: Using let

```
let age = 25;
console.log(age); // Output: 25

age = 30; // Allowed (Reassignment)
```

```
console.log(age); // Output: 30

let age = 40; // ❌ Error! Cannot redeclare 'age' in the same scope
```

3. const (Constant Values)

- **Variables declared with const cannot be reassigned or redeclared.**
- **They are block-scoped like let.**
- **They must be initialized when declared.**

Example: Using const

```
const country = "India";
console.log(country); // Output: India

country = "USA"; // ❌ Error! Cannot reassign a constant variable
```

14.1.2 Comparison Table

Feature	var	let	const
Reassignable?	☑ Yes	☑ Yes	❌ No
Redeclarable?	☑ Yes	❌ No	❌ No
Scope	Function-scoped	Block-scoped	Block-scoped
Hoisted?	☑ Yes (but undefined)	☑ Yes (but not initialized)	☑ Yes (but not initialized)

14.1.3 Use Case

Scenario	Use var?	Use let?	Use const?
Declaring a variable inside a function	☑ Yes	☑ Yes	❌ No
Storing a value that won't change (e.g., PI value)	❌ No	❌ No	☑ Yes
Loop counters (for loops)	❌ No	☑ Yes	❌ No

14.2 Arrow Functions

Arrow functions (=>) provide a shorter way to write functions.

14.2.1 Traditional Function vs Arrow Function
Example: Regular Function

```
function greet(name) {
    return "Hello, " + name;
}
console.log(greet("John")); // Output: Hello, John
```

Example: Arrow Function

```
const greet = (name) => "Hello, " + name;
console.log(greet("John")); // Output: Hello, John
```

14.2.2 When to Use Arrow Functions?

- *When writing short functions*
- *When you don't need this keyword inside the function*

14.3 Spread and Rest Operators

The **spread (...)** and **rest (...)** operators look the same but have different purposes.

14.3.1 Spread Operator (...)

The spread operator **expands** an array or object.

Example: Copying an Array

```
let numbers = [1, 2, 3];
let newNumbers = [...numbers, 4, 5];

console.log(newNumbers); // Output: [1, 2, 3, 4, 5]
```

Example: Merging Objects

```
let person = { name: "Alice", age: 25 };
let newPerson = { ...person, city: "New York" };

console.log(newPerson); // Output: { name: "Alice", age: 25, city: "New York" }
```

14.3.2 Rest Operator (...)

The rest operator **collects** multiple values into an array.

Example: Using Rest in Function Parameters

```javascript
function sum(...numbers) {
    return numbers.reduce((total, num) => total + num, 0);
}
console.log(sum(1, 2, 3, 4)); // Output: 10
```

14.4 Destructuring Assignment

Destructuring lets you **extract values from arrays or objects** easily.

14.4.1 Array Destructuring
Example: Extracting Values from an Array

```javascript
let colors = ["Red", "Green", "Blue"];
let [first, second, third] = colors;

console.log(first); // Output: Red
console.log(second); // Output: Green
console.log(third); // Output: Blue
```

14.4.2 Object Destructuring
Example: Extracting Values from an Object

```javascript
let user = { name: "John", age: 30 };
let { name, age } = user;

console.log(name); // Output: John
console.log(age); // Output: 30
```

$$\overline{}$$

Assignment - Hour 14

1. Convert the following function into an arrow function:

```
function multiply(a, b) {
    return a * b;
}
```

2. Use the spread operator to merge these two objects:

```
let obj1 = { a: 1, b: 2 };
let obj2 = { c: 3, d: 4 };
```

3. Use destructuring to extract values from this array:

```
let fruits = ["Apple", "Banana", "Mango"];
```

Short Answer Questions

1. What is the difference between var, let, and const?
2. Why is let preferred over var?
3. What is the main advantage of arrow functions?
4. How do you use the spread operator with arrays?
5. What does the rest operator do?
6. How does destructuring simplify code?
7. Can you reassign a variable declared with const?
8. What happens if you redeclare a let variable?
9. How do you copy an object using the spread operator?
10. What will be the output of the following code?

```
const [x, y] = [10, 20];
console.log(x, y);
```

This hour provides a **strong foundation in modern JavaScript features** that make coding easier and more efficient.

Hour 15
Introduction to
Asynchronous JavaScript

15.1 What is Asynchronous JavaScript?

In JavaScript, code is usually executed **line by line, from top to bottom**. This is called **synchronous execution**. However, sometimes we need to perform tasks that take time, like:

- Fetching data from the internet
- Reading a file from a computer
- Waiting for user input

If JavaScript waited for each task to finish before moving to the next, the whole program would **freeze**. To solve this, JavaScript has an **asynchronous** feature that allows it to **continue running other code** while waiting for time-consuming tasks to complete.

15.1.1 Understanding Synchronous vs Asynchronous Code

Let's compare both with examples:

Synchronous Code Example

```
console.log("Start");
console.log("Middle");
console.log("End");
```

Output:

```
Start
Middle
End
```

Here, the execution happens in order—**one line at a time**.

Asynchronous Code Example

```
console.log("Start");

setTimeout(() => {
  console.log("Middle");
}, 2000); // 2 seconds delay

console.log("End");
```

Output:

```
Start
End
Middle
```

Here's what happens:
1. Start is printed first.
2. setTimeout is called, but JavaScript does not **wait** for it to finish. It moves to the next line.
3. End is printed immediately.
4. After **2 seconds**, Middle is printed.

This is called **non-blocking execution**, which makes JavaScript **fast and efficient**.

15.2 Callbacks: The Old Way of Handling Asynchronous Tasks

15.2.1 What is a Callback?

A **callback** is a function passed as an **argument** to another function, to be executed later.

15.2.2 Example of a Callback Function

```javascript
function greet(name, callback) {
  console.log("Hello, " + name);
  callback();
}

function sayGoodbye() {
  console.log("Goodbye!");
}

greet("John", sayGoodbye);
```

Output:

```
Hello, John
Goodbye!
```

Here's what happens:
1. greet("John", sayGoodbye) is called.
2. "Hello, John" is printed.
3. The sayGoodbye function is called inside greet, printing "Goodbye!".

15.2.3 Callbacks in Asynchronous JavaScript

We often use callbacks when working with **asynchronous functions**, like fetching data from the internet.

```javascript
function fetchData(callback) {
  setTimeout(() => {
    console.log("Data fetched from server");
    callback();
  }, 2000);
}

function processData() {
  console.log("Processing data...");
}

fetchData(processData);
```

Output:

```
Data fetched from server
Processing data...
```

15.2.4 Problems with Callbacks – Callback Hell

When multiple callbacks are **nested inside each other**, the code becomes **hard to read**. This is called **callback hell**.

```javascript
setTimeout(() => {
  console.log("Step 1 complete");
  setTimeout(() => {
    console.log("Step 2 complete");
    setTimeout(() => {
      console.log("Step 3 complete");
    }, 1000);
  }, 1000);
}, 1000);
```

Output: (each step after 1 second)

```
Step 1 complete
Step 2 complete
Step 3 complete
```

This is messy! **Promises** solve this problem.

15.3 Promises: A Better Way to Handle Asynchronous Tasks
15.3.1 What is a Promise?

A **Promise** is an object that represents a value that may be available **now, later, or never**.

A Promise has **three states**:
1. **Pending** – The task is still running.
2. **Resolved (Fulfilled)** – The task is successful.
3. **Rejected** – The task failed.

15.3.2 Creating a Promise

```javascript
let myPromise = new Promise((resolve, reject) => {
  let success = true;
  if (success) {
    resolve("Task completed!");
  } else {
    reject("Task failed.");
  }
});


console.log(myPromise);
```

Output:

```
Promise {<resolved>: "Task completed!"}
```

15.3.3 Using .then() with Promises

```javascript
let myPromise = new Promise((resolve, reject) => {
  setTimeout(() => {
    resolve("Data received!");
  }, 2000);
});


myPromise.then((message) => {
  console.log(message);
});
```

Output after 2 seconds:

```
Data received!
```

15.3.4 Using .catch() for Error Handling

```javascript
let myPromise = new Promise((resolve, reject) => {
```

```javascript
  setTimeout(() => {
    reject("Error: Data not found!");
  }, 2000);
});

myPromise
  .then((message) => console.log(message))
  .catch((error) => console.log(error));
```

Output after 2 seconds:

```
Error: Data not found!
```

15.4 Async/Await: The Modern Way of Handling Asynchronous Tasks
15.4.1 What is Async/Await?

- **async** makes a function return a Promise.
- **await** waits for the Promise to resolve before moving to the next line.

15.4.2 Using async and await

```javascript
async function fetchData() {
  return "Data retrieved!";
}

fetchData().then(console.log);
```

Output:

```
Data retrieved!
```

15.4.3 Using await Inside an Async Function

```javascript
function delay() {
  return new Promise(resolve => setTimeout(resolve, 2000));
}

async function fetchData() {
  console.log("Fetching data...");
  await delay();
  console.log("Data received!");
}

fetchData();
```

Output:

```
Fetching data...
(Data appears after 2 seconds)
Data received!
```

15.4.4 Handling Errors in Async/Await

```
async function fetchData() {
  try {
    throw new Error("Network Error");
  } catch (error) {
    console.log(error.message);
  }
}

fetchData();
```

Output:

```
Network Error
```

15.5 Use Case: Fetching API Data

```
async function getUserData() {
  let response = await
fetch("https://jsonplaceholder.typicode.com/users/1");
  let data = await response.json();
  console.log(data);
}

getUserData();
```

Output:

```
(User details in JSON format)
```

Practical Exercises

1. Write a function using callback to print "Hello" after 3 seconds.
2. Create a Promise that resolves with "Success!" after 1 second and use .then() to print the message.
3. Write an async/await function to wait 2 seconds before printing "Async function executed!".

Practice Questions

1. What is synchronous and asynchronous execution?
2. What is the purpose of setTimeout()?
3. What is a callback function?
4. What is "callback hell"?
5. What are the three states of a Promise?
6. How do we handle errors in Promises?
7. What does async do?
8. Why is await useful?
9. What is the difference between .then() and await?
10. Why is async/await preferred over callbacks?

This structure ensures **step-by-step learning with examples, outputs, and exercises**.

Hour 16
Fetch API and Working with JSON

Introduction

JavaScript is widely used for building websites and web applications. But how do we get real-world data from the internet into our JavaScript programs? That's where the **Fetch API** and **JSON (JavaScript Object Notation)** come in!

In this hour, we will learn:

1. How to make HTTP requests using the **Fetch API**.
2. How to handle and process responses from APIs.
3. How to work with **JSON data** in JavaScript.

By the end of this hour, you will be able to fetch real-time data from the internet and display it on a webpage.

16.1 Making HTTP Requests with Fetch
16.1.1 What is the Fetch API?

The **Fetch API** is a built-in JavaScript feature that allows us to request and retrieve data from a server (like a website or API). It is commonly used to get data from external sources such as weather apps, stock market apps, and more.

Think of it like ordering food online:

- You (the client) **request** a meal from a restaurant (server).
- The restaurant processes your order and **responds** with the meal (data).
- You receive the food and enjoy it!

Similarly, the Fetch API sends a request to a server, waits for a response, and then retrieves the data.

16.1.2 Basic Syntax of Fetch

The Fetch API uses the fetch() function, which returns a **Promise** (a special type of JavaScript object that handles asynchronous operations).

Syntax:

```
fetch(URL)
  .then(response => response.json())
  .then(data => console.log(data))
  .catch(error => console.log("Error:", error));
```

- fetch(URL): Sends a request to the given URL.

- .then(response => response.json()): Converts the response into JSON format.
- .then(data => console.log(data)): Logs the data to the console.
- .catch(error => console.log("Error:", error)): Catches any errors that may occur.

16.1.3 Example: Fetching Data from an API

Let's fetch data from a free API that provides random user details.
Code Example:

```
fetch("https://randomuser.me/api/")
  .then(response => response.json())
  .then(data => console.log(data))
  .catch(error => console.log("Error:", error));
```

Expected Output (Example Response):

```
{
  "results": [
    {
      "name": { "title": "Mr", "first": "John", "last": "Doe" },
      "email": "johndoe@example.com",
      "location": { "city": "New York", "country": "USA" }
    }
  ]
}
```

16.2 Handling API Responses
16.2.1 What is an API Response?

When we request data using fetch(), the server sends back a **response**. This response contains:

1. **Status Code** (e.g., 200 for success, 404 for not found).
2. **Headers** (metadata about the response).
3. **Body** (the actual data, usually in JSON format).

Common HTTP Status Codes

Status Code	Meaning
200	Success
201	Created
400	Bad Request

Status Code	Meaning
401	Unauthorized
404	Not Found
500	Internal Server Error

16.2.2 Checking for Errors in Fetch API

If something goes wrong (e.g., the API is down), we need to **handle errors** properly.

Example: Handling Errors

```javascript
fetch("https://randomuser.me/api/")
 .then(response => {
  if (!response.ok) {
    throw new Error("Network response was not OK");
  }
  return response.json();
})
.then(data => console.log(data))
.catch(error => console.log("Fetch error:", error));
```

- The if (!response.ok) checks if the request was successful.
- If not, we use throw new Error() to handle it.
- .catch(error => console.log("Fetch error:", error)) displays the error message.

16.3 Parsing and Displaying JSON Data
16.3.1 What is JSON?

JSON (JavaScript Object Notation) is a format for storing and transporting data. It looks similar to JavaScript objects.
Example JSON Data:

```json
{
  "name": "Alice",
  "age": 25,
  "city": "London"
}
```

Converting JSON to JavaScript Object:

```javascript
let jsonData = '{"name": "Alice", "age": 25, "city": "London"}';
```

```javascript
let obj = JSON.parse(jsonData);
console.log(obj.name); // Output: Alice
```
Converting JavaScript Object to JSON:
```javascript
let user = { name: "Bob", age: 30, city: "Paris" };
let jsonString = JSON.stringify(user);
console.log(jsonString);
```

16.3.2 Displaying JSON Data in HTML

Let's display fetched data on a webpage.

Example: Fetch User Data and Display It

```javascript
fetch("https://randomuser.me/api/")
  .then(response => response.json())
  .then(data => {
   let user = data.results[0];
   document.getElementById("user-info").innerHTML = `
    <h2>${user.name.first} ${user.name.last}</h2>
    <p>Email: ${user.email}</p>
    <p>Location: ${user.location.city}, ${user.location.country}</p>
   `;
 })
  .catch(error => console.log("Error:", error));
```

HTML Part:

```html
<div id="user-info"></div>
```

Use Cases of Fetch API and JSON
1. **Weather Apps** – Fetch real-time weather data.
2. **News Websites** – Display the latest headlines from a news API.
3. **Stock Market Apps** – Get live stock prices.

Exercise 1: Fetch Random Dog Images

Write a JavaScript program to fetch a random dog image from the API:
https://dog.ceo/api/breeds/image/random
Display it inside an <img> tag in HTML.

Exercise 2: Fetch and Display Jokes

Write a program to fetch a random joke from https://official-joke-api.appspot.com/random_joke
Display the joke on a webpage.

Exercise 3: Fetch and Search User Data

Modify the random user API example to allow users to **search** for a user by country.

Short Answer Questions - Hour 16

1. What is the Fetch API?
2. What does .then() do in the Fetch API?
3. How do you handle errors in Fetch?
4. What is JSON?
5. How do you convert JSON data into a JavaScript object?
6. What does fetch("URL") return?
7. What are some real-life use cases of Fetch API?
8. How do you display fetched data on a webpage?
9. What is an API?
10. How do you check if an API response is successful?

This was **Hour 16: Fetch API and Working with JSON**. Hope you understood it well!

Hour 17
JavaScript and Local Storage

17.1 What is LocalStorage and SessionStorage?
17.1.1 Introduction to Web Storage

When you visit a website, the website may need to **store some data** on your browser so that it can remember your preferences or settings. For example, a shopping site may save your cart items so that they are still there when you come back later.

JavaScript provides a feature called **Web Storage**, which helps store data **inside the user's browser**. There are two types of web storage:

1. **LocalStorage** – Stores data permanently in the browser until the user manually deletes it.
2. **SessionStorage** – Stores data temporarily and deletes it when the browser is closed.

17.1.2 Difference Between LocalStorage and SessionStorage

Feature	LocalStorage	SessionStorage
Data Persistence	Data remains **even after closing the browser**.	Data is **deleted when the browser is closed**.
Storage Limit	Up to **5MB** of data.	Up to **5MB** of data.
Accessibility	Accessible by **all pages** from the same origin (same website).	Accessible **only within the same session** (tab).

17.2 Storing and Retrieving Data
17.2.1 Using LocalStorage

LocalStorage allows us to **store key-value pairs** in the browser, which remain **even after the page is refreshed or the browser is closed**.

17.2.1.1 Storing Data in LocalStorage

To store data, we use the localStorage.setItem() method.
Example: Storing a Name in LocalStorage

```
localStorage.setItem("username", "John");
console.log("Data stored in LocalStorage!");
```

Output (stored in browser memory):
Data stored in LocalStorage!

17.2.1.2 Retrieving Data from LocalStorage

To get the stored value, we use the localStorage.getItem() method.

Example: Retrieving the Name from LocalStorage

```
let name = localStorage.getItem("username");
console.log("Welcome, " + name + "!");
```

```
Output:
Welcome, John!
```

17.2.1.3 Removing Data from LocalStorage

We can remove a single item using localStorage.removeItem().

Example: Removing the Name from LocalStorage

```
localStorage.removeItem("username");
console.log("Username removed from LocalStorage!");
```

```
Output:
Username removed from LocalStorage!
To clear all stored data, use localStorage.clear().
```

Example: Clearing All Data from LocalStorage

```
localStorage.clear();
console.log("All data cleared from LocalStorage!");
```

```
Output:
All data cleared from LocalStorage!
```

17.2.2 Using SessionStorage

SessionStorage works similarly to LocalStorage, but the data disappears **once the browser is closed**.

17.2.2.1 Storing Data in SessionStorage

```
sessionStorage.setItem("city", "New York");
console.log("City stored in SessionStorage!");
```

```
Output:
City stored in SessionStorage!
```

17.2.2.2 Retrieving Data from SessionStorage

```
let city = sessionStorage.getItem("city");
console.log("You are in " + city);
```

Output:
You are in New York

17.2.2.3 Removing Data from SessionStorage

```
sessionStorage.removeItem("city");
console.log("City removed from SessionStorage!");
```

Output:
City removed from SessionStorage!

17.3 Use Cases for LocalStorage
17.3.1 Use Case 1: Saving User Preferences (Theme Selection)

A website can **remember the user's theme selection** (light or dark mode) using LocalStorage.

Example: Storing User's Preferred Theme

```
localStorage.setItem("theme", "dark");
console.log("Theme preference saved!");
```

When the user **reopens the website**, we can retrieve the theme and apply it.

```
let theme = localStorage.getItem("theme");
console.log("User prefers " + theme + " mode.");
```

Output:
User prefers dark mode.

17.3.2 Use Case 2: Storing Shopping Cart Items

E-commerce websites use LocalStorage to **remember items added to the cart**.

Example: Saving Items to Cart

```
let cart = ["Laptop", "Mouse", "Keyboard"];
localStorage.setItem("cartItems", JSON.stringify(cart));
console.log("Cart items saved!");
```

Output:
Cart items saved!

To retrieve the stored items:

```javascript
let savedCart = JSON.parse(localStorage.getItem("cartItems"));
console.log("Your Cart:", savedCart);
```

Output:
Your Cart: ["Laptop", "Mouse", "Keyboard"]

17.3.3 Use Case 3: Auto-Saving Form Data

If a user fills out a form and accidentally **refreshes the page**, LocalStorage can save the data.

Example: Saving and Retrieving Form Data

```javascript
document.querySelector("#nameField").addEventListener("input",
function (e) {
   localStorage.setItem("formName", e.target.value);
});

window.onload = function () {
   document.querySelector("#nameField").value =
localStorage.getItem("formName") || "";
};
```

☑ **Behavior:**

- When typing in the field, the name is **automatically saved**.
- When the page refreshes, the name is **restored** from LocalStorage.

Practical Exercises

1. **Create a simple to-do list app** using LocalStorage to save tasks even after the page is refreshed.
2. **Make a theme switcher** (light/dark mode) where the selection is stored in LocalStorage.
3. **Develop a form autosave feature** that keeps entered text saved even if the user accidentally refreshes the page.

17.5 Short Answer Type Questions

1. What is LocalStorage in JavaScript?
2. How does SessionStorage differ from LocalStorage?
3. How can you store and retrieve data from LocalStorage?
4. How do you delete a single item from LocalStorage?
5. What happens to data in SessionStorage when the browser is closed?
6. Why do we use JSON.stringify() and JSON.parse() with LocalStorage?
7. How can LocalStorage help in creating a theme switcher?
8. What is the storage limit of LocalStorage?
9. Can LocalStorage store JavaScript objects directly? Why or why not?
10. Write the JavaScript code to store and retrieve a user's age from LocalStorage.

This chapter ensures **complete beginners** understand LocalStorage and SessionStorage with **clear explanations, examples, use cases, and practical exercises**.

Hour 18
Object-Oriented Programming (OOP) in JavaScript

Understanding Classes, Objects, Constructors, Inheritance, and Prototypes

18.1 Introduction to Object-Oriented Programming (OOP)

Object-Oriented Programming (OOP) is a way of writing code that organizes data and behavior into reusable structures called **objects**. It helps in building complex applications efficiently.

18.1.1 What is an Object?

An **object** is a collection of **properties** (variables) and **methods** (functions). Think of a real-world object, like a **car**:

- It has **properties** (color, brand, speed).
- It has **methods** (drive, brake, honk).

In JavaScript, objects are created using **curly braces {}**:

```javascript
let car = {
  brand: "Toyota",
  color: "Red",
  speed: 120,
  drive: function() {
    console.log("The car is driving at " + this.speed + " km/h.");
  }
};


console.log(car.brand); // Output: Toyota
car.drive(); // Output: The car is driving at 120 km/h.
```

18.1.2 Why Use OOP?

OOP helps in:

- **Reusability** – Write code once and reuse it.
- **Modularity** – Keep the code organized.
- **Scalability** – Easily extend the code for bigger applications.

18.2 Creating Classes and Objects

A **class** is a blueprint for creating multiple objects with the same properties and methods.

18.2.1 Creating a Class

A class is defined using the class keyword:

```javascript
class Car {
  constructor(brand, color, speed) {
    this.brand = brand;
    this.color = color;
    this.speed = speed;
  }

  drive() {
    console.log(`${this.brand} is driving at ${this.speed} km/h.`);
  }
}

// Creating objects
let car1 = new Car("Toyota", "Red", 120);
let car2 = new Car("Honda", "Blue", 100);

console.log(car1.brand); // Output: Toyota
car1.drive(); // Output: Toyota is driving at 120 km/h.

console.log(car2.color); // Output: Blue
car2.drive(); // Output: Honda is driving at 100 km/h.
```

18.2.2 Understanding the Constructor Method

- The **constructor** is a special function inside a class that initializes object properties.
- It runs automatically when an object is created.

Use Case: Creating a Bank Account System

A bank system where each customer has an **account number, balance, and deposit method**.

```javascript
class BankAccount {
  constructor(accountNumber, balance) {
    this.accountNumber = accountNumber;
    this.balance = balance;
  }

  deposit(amount) {
    this.balance += amount;
```

```
    console.log(`Deposited $${amount}. New balance: $${this.balance}`);
  }
}

// Creating accounts
let account1 = new BankAccount(12345, 500);
account1.deposit(200); // Output: Deposited $200. New balance:
$700
```

18.3 Constructor Functions (Old Way of Creating Classes)

Before ES6 classes, objects were created using **constructor functions**.

```
function Person(name, age) {
  this.name = name;
  this.age = age;
  this.greet = function() {
    console.log(`Hello, my name is ${this.name}.`);
  };
}

let person1 = new Person("Alice", 25);
person1.greet(); // Output: Hello, my name is Alice.
```

Even though classes are preferred in modern JavaScript, older codebases still use constructor functions.

18.4 Inheritance – Extending a Class

Inheritance allows a class to reuse properties and methods of another class.

18.4.1 Creating a Subclass

A **child class** can extend a **parent class** using the extends keyword.

```
class Animal {
  constructor(name) {
    this.name = name;
  }

  makeSound() {
    console.log(`${this.name} makes a sound.`);
  }
}

class Dog extends Animal {
```

```javascript
  bark() {
    console.log(`${this.name} barks.`);
  }
}

let dog1 = new Dog("Buddy");
dog1.makeSound(); // Output: Buddy makes a sound.
dog1.bark(); // Output: Buddy barks.
```

Use Case: Employee Management System

```javascript
class Employee {
  constructor(name, salary) {
    this.name = name;
    this.salary = salary;
  }

  showDetails() {
    console.log(`${this.name} earns $${this.salary} per month.`);
  }
}

class Manager extends Employee {
  constructor(name, salary, department) {
    super(name, salary);
    this.department = department;
  }

  showDetails() {
    console.log(`${this.name} manages the ${this.department}
department.`);
  }
}

let emp1 = new Employee("John", 3000);
emp1.showDetails(); // Output: John earns $3000 per month.

let mgr1 = new Manager("Alice", 5000, "Sales");
mgr1.showDetails(); // Output: Alice manages the Sales
department.
```

18.5 JavaScript Prototypes

JavaScript uses **prototypes** instead of classes internally. Every object inherits properties from its prototype.

18.5.1 Adding Methods to Prototype

```javascript
function Person(name) {
  this.name = name;
}

Person.prototype.greet = function() {
  console.log(`Hello, my name is ${this.name}.`);
};

let person2 = new Person("Mike");
person2.greet(); // Output: Hello, my name is Mike.
```

18.5.2 Why Use Prototypes?

- Saves memory: Functions are not duplicated for each object.
- Used internally by JavaScript for inheritance.

18.6 Summary Table: OOP in JavaScript

Concept	Explanation	Example
Object	A collection of properties and methods	{ name: "Car", speed: 100 }
Class	A blueprint for creating objects	class Car {}
Constructor	Initializes object properties	constructor(brand) { this.brand = brand; }
Inheritance	Allows a class to extend another class	class Dog extends Animal {}
Prototype	A way to add methods to objects	Person.prototype.greet = function() {}

Solve the following exercises using JavaScript:

1. **Create a Student Class**
   - Properties: name, age, grade
   - Method: displayDetails()
   - Create two students and display their details.
2. **Create a Library System**
   - Class: Book
   - Properties: title, author, year
   - Method: bookInfo()
   - Create two books and display their information.
3. **Create an Animal Inheritance System**
   - Parent Class: Animal (property: name, method: makeSound())
   - Child Class: Dog (method: bark())
   - Create a dog object and call both methods.

Short Answer Questions

1. What is an object in JavaScript?
2. How do you create a class in JavaScript?
3. What is a constructor method used for?
4. How do you create an object from a class?
5. What is inheritance in JavaScript?
6. What does the extends keyword do?
7. What is a prototype in JavaScript?
8. How do you add a method to a prototype?
9. What is the difference between a class and a prototype?
10. Why is OOP useful in JavaScript?

This concludes **Hour 18** of learning JavaScript. We are now proceeding to **Hour 19: JavaScript Modules and Imports**!

JS

Hour 19
JavaScript Modules and Imports

A Beginner-Friendly Guide with Practical Examples

19.1 Understanding Modules in JavaScript
19.1.1 What Are Modules?

In JavaScript, a **module** is a separate file that contains reusable code. Instead of writing all your JavaScript in one big file, you can **split** your code into multiple files and use them where needed. This makes your code **organized, easier to maintain, and reusable**.

Think of a module like a **toolbox**. Instead of carrying all your tools in your hand, you keep them in different boxes. When you need a tool, you take it from the correct box. Similarly, in JavaScript, you **import** the necessary module instead of writing the same code again and again.

19.1.2 Why Use Modules?

Here are some benefits of using modules in JavaScript:

Feature	Description
Code Reusability	You can write a function once and use it in multiple files.
Better Organization	Code is split into logical parts, making it easier to manage.
Avoiding Conflicts	Variables and functions in one module won't affect others.
Improved Readability	Small, separate files are easier to understand than one large file.

19.1.3 Example Without Modules (Messy Code)

If we don't use modules, all functions are in the same file:

```javascript
function add(a, b) {
   return a + b;
}

function subtract(a, b) {
   return a - b;
}
```

```
console.log(add(5, 3));  // Output: 8
console.log(subtract(10, 4));  // Output: 6
```

This approach **works** but becomes **messy** when the project grows. Instead, let's use modules.

19.2 Importing and Exporting Functions
19.2.1 Creating a Module (Exporting a Function)

To create a module, we write code in a separate file and **export** it.

[1] **Create a file called math.js and add this code:**

```
export function add(a, b) {
   return a + b;
}

export function subtract(a, b) {
   return a - b;
}
```

Here, export makes these functions **available** for use in other files.

19.2.2 Using the Module (Importing a Function)

[2] **Create another file called main.js and import the functions:**

```
import { add, subtract } from './math.js';

console.log(add(5, 3));  // Output: 8
console.log(subtract(10, 4));  // Output: 6
```

- **What Happened?**
  - import { add, subtract } from './math.js' brings the functions from math.js into main.js.
  - Now we can use add() and subtract() without rewriting them.

19.2.3 Exporting Everything at Once

Instead of exporting functions separately, we can export them together:
math.js

```
function add(a, b) {
   return a + b;
}
```

```javascript
function subtract(a, b) {
  return a - b;
}

export { add, subtract };
```

main.js

```javascript
import * as MathFunctions from './math.js';

console.log(MathFunctions.add(7, 2));  // Output: 9
console.log(MathFunctions.subtract(10, 4));  // Output: 6
```

◆ import * as MathFunctions means **import everything** from math.js and use it with MathFunctions.add().

19.3 Using JavaScript Modules in Web Development
19.3.1 Using Modules in an HTML File

When using JavaScript in a **webpage**, we must include type="module":

index.html

```html
<!DOCTYPE html>
<html>
<head>
  <title>JavaScript Modules</title>
</head>
<body>
  <script type="module" src="main.js"></script>
</body>
</html>
```

Now, JavaScript modules will work in the browser.

19.3.2 Real-World Use Case: Fetching API Data

Let's use modules to **fetch user data from an API**.

api.js

```javascript
export async function fetchUser() {
  let response = await
fetch('https://jsonplaceholder.typicode.com/users/1');
  let user = await response.json();
  return user;
}
```

📁 main.js

```js
import { fetchUser } from './api.js';

fetchUser().then(user => console.log(user));
```

- This makes our code **clean** and **modular**, following best practices.

1. Create a module **greet.js** that exports a function greet(name) which prints "Hello, name!". Import and use it in another file.
2. Create a module **math.js** that exports functions for multiplication and division. Import them and use them in main.js.
3. Create a module that fetches and displays the title of a post from https://jsonplaceholder.typicode.com/posts/1.

Short Answer Questions

1. What is a module in JavaScript?
2. How do you export a function from a JavaScript module?
3. What is the syntax to import a specific function from a module?
4. Why do we use type="module" in an HTML file?
5. What is the difference between named exports and default exports?
6. How do you import everything from a module?
7. How do JavaScript modules help in better code organization?
8. Can you use JavaScript modules in Node.js?
9. What will happen if you forget to use type="module" in an HTML file?
10. What are the advantages of using JavaScript modules?

This structured content ensures **complete beginners** can understand JavaScript modules with **step-by-step explanations, examples, and real-world use cases**.

20.1 What Are JavaScript Frameworks?

20.1.1 Understanding Frameworks in Simple Terms

Imagine you are building a house. You have two options:

1. **Start from scratch**, making bricks, mixing cement, and designing everything yourself.
2. **Use a pre-built structure**, where the foundation and walls are already set up, and you just need to decorate.

JavaScript frameworks work like the second option. Instead of writing every line of code manually, a **JavaScript framework** gives you a ready-made structure to build web applications **faster and easier**.

Definition:

A **JavaScript framework** is a collection of **pre-written JavaScript code** that helps developers build web applications quickly by providing built-in functions, components, and tools.

20.1.2 Why Use a JavaScript Framework?

JavaScript frameworks help in many ways:

- ☑ **Faster Development** – Pre-built functions save time.

- ☑ **Less Code Writing** – Common tasks (like updating a webpage) are easier.
- ☑ **Better Performance** – Code runs efficiently.
- ☑ **Easy Maintenance** – Frameworks follow best practices, making updates easier.
- ☑ **Community Support** – Many people contribute, so you get help easily.

20.2 Overview of JavaScript Frameworks

JavaScript has many frameworks, but three of the most popular are:

1. **React** – Developed by Facebook, great for interactive UIs.
2. **Vue.js** – Lightweight and easy to learn.
3. **Angular** – Developed by Google, best for large applications.

20.2.1 React.js – A Beginner-Friendly Overview

React is a **component-based library** (often called a framework) created by Facebook. It allows developers to **break down a webpage into small reusable components**, making it easier to manage.

Example: A Simple React Component

Below is an example of a simple **React component** that displays a message:

```
import React from 'react';

function Greeting() {
  return <h1>Hello, welcome to React!</h1>;
}


export default Greeting;
```

Output:

(When rendered in a React application, the browser will show:)
Hello, welcome to React!

Why Choose React?

- ☑ **Reusable Components** – Build once, use anywhere.
- ☑ **Fast Rendering** – Uses Virtual DOM for speed.
- ☑ **Strong Community** – Used by Facebook and many companies.

20.2.2 Vue.js – The Beginner-Friendly Framework

Vue.js is a **lightweight** and **easy-to-learn** framework, great for beginners. It is simpler than React and Angular but powerful enough for most applications.

Example: A Simple Vue Component

Here's how to create a **Vue component** that shows a message:

```
<div id="app">
  <h1>{{ message }}</h1>
</div>

<script>
  const app = Vue.createApp({
    data() {
      return {
        message: "Hello, welcome to Vue.js!"
```

```
    };
  }
});
app.mount("#app");
</script>
```

Output:

```
Hello, welcome to Vue.js!
```

Why Choose Vue.js?

- ☑ **Very Easy to Learn** – Simple syntax.
- ☑ **Lightweight and Fast** – Small size, loads quickly.
- ☑ **Two-Way Binding** – Changes in UI update data automatically.

20.2.3 Angular – The Full-Fledged Framework

Angular is a **powerful framework** developed by Google, used for building **large-scale web applications**.

Example: A Simple Angular Component

Below is a basic **Angular component** that displays a message:

```
import { Component } from '@angular/core';

@Component({
  selector: 'app-greeting',
  template: '<h1>{{ message }}</h1>'
})
export class GreetingComponent {
  message: string = 'Hello, welcome to Angular!';
}
```

Output:

```
Hello, welcome to Angular!
```

Why Choose Angular?

- ☑ **Best for Large Applications** – Used by Google, Microsoft, and IBM.
- ☑ **Complete Framework** – Comes with everything you need.
- ☑ **Great for Teams** – Well-structured and scalable.

20.3 When to Use Vanilla JavaScript vs Frameworks

Now that you know about frameworks, the big question is: **When should you use a framework, and when should you use plain JavaScript (Vanilla JavaScript)?**

Feature	Vanilla JavaScript	Frameworks (React, Vue, Angular)
Ease of Learning	Easier for small projects	Easier for large projects
Performance	Fast for small projects	Faster for complex apps
Code Structure	Manual organization	Pre-defined structure
Best For	Simple websites, small tasks	Complex web applications

20.3.1 When to Use Vanilla JavaScript?

- When making **small projects** like a personal webpage.
- When **performance** is the top priority.
- When **learning JavaScript basics** before frameworks.

20.3.2 When to Use a Framework?

- When building **large applications** like social media sites.
- When working **in a team** (frameworks help organize code).
- When using **modern web features** like single-page applications (SPA).

Practical Exercises

1. **Create a simple webpage using Vanilla JavaScript** that changes the background color when clicking a button.
2. **Build a basic React component** that displays "Hello, [Your Name]" dynamically.
3. **Make a simple Vue.js app** that takes user input and displays it on the screen.

Short Answer Questions (Hour 20)

1. What is a JavaScript framework?
2. Name three popular JavaScript frameworks.
3. How does React differ from Vue.js?
4. What is a component in React?
5. Why is Vue.js considered beginner-friendly?
6. What company developed Angular?
7. When should you use Vanilla JavaScript instead of a framework?
8. What does two-way data binding mean in Vue.js?
9. What is the main advantage of using a JavaScript framework?
10. What does "SPA" stand for in web development?

This completes **Hour 20: Introduction to JavaScript Frameworks**

Hour 21
Building a Simple
Web Application

In this hour, we will learn how to build a simple web application using **HTML, CSS, and JavaScript**. We will start from scratch, ensuring that even a complete beginner can follow along.

By the end of this lesson, you will be able to:

- ☑ **Set up a basic web project** (HTML, CSS, and JavaScript).
- ☑ **Handle user input dynamically** using JavaScript.
- ☑ **Display data dynamically on a webpage.**

Let's get started!

21.1 Setting Up an HTML/CSS/JS Project

Before we start coding, we need to set up a basic **web development environment**.

21.1.1 What is a Web Application?

A **web application** is a program that runs in a web browser. It is made up of three main parts:

Technology	Purpose
HTML (HyperText Markup Language)	Structure of the webpage (headings, buttons, text, etc.)
CSS (Cascading Style Sheets)	Styles the webpage (colors, fonts, layouts)
JavaScript	Adds interactivity (handling button clicks, updating content dynamically)

21.1.2 Creating Your First Web Project

We will create a **simple web project** with three files:

1. **index.html** → The structure of the page
2. **style.css** → The design (colors, fonts, layout)
3. **script.js** → The logic (handling user input, updating content dynamically)

Step 1: Create a Project Folder

✦ Create a new folder on your computer called **MyWebApp**.

Step 2: Create HTML File

Inside the **MyWebApp** folder, create a file called **index.html** and add the following code:

```html
<!DOCTYPE html>
<html lang="en">
<head>
  <meta charset="UTF-8">
  <meta name="viewport" content="width=device-width, initial-scale=1.0">
  <title>My First Web App</title>
  <link rel="stylesheet" href="style.css">
</head>
<body>
  <h1>Welcome to My Web App</h1>
  <p>Enter your name:</p>
  <input type="text" id="nameInput">
  <button onclick="displayMessage()">Submit</button>
  <p id="message"></p>

  <script src="script.js"></script>
</body>
</html>
```

✓ Explanation:
- We created a basic HTML page with a **heading**, a **text input**, a **button**, and a **paragraph** to display a message.
- We linked a **CSS file (style.css)** to style our page.
- We linked a **JavaScript file (script.js)** to add interactivity.

Step 3: Create CSS File

Now, create a file called **style.css** inside the **MyWebApp** folder and add the following code:

```css
body {
  font-family: Arial, sans-serif;
  text-align: center;
  margin-top: 50px;
}

input {
  padding: 5px;
```

```css
    margin: 10px;
}

button {
    padding: 8px 15px;
    background-color: blue;
    color: white;
    border: none;
    cursor: pointer;
}

button:hover {
    background-color: darkblue;
}
```

✓ Explanation:

- We set a **font** for the page and **centered** all text.
- We styled the **input box** and **button** to look better.
- We added a **hover effect** to the button (it changes color when the user moves the mouse over it).

Step 4: Create JavaScript File

Now, create a file called **script.js** and add the following code:

```javascript
function displayMessage() {
    let name = document.getElementById("nameInput").value;
    let message = document.getElementById("message");

    if (name.trim() === "") {
        message.innerHTML = "Please enter your name!";
        message.style.color = "red";
    } else {
        message.innerHTML = "Hello, " + name + "! Welcome to My Web
App!";
        message.style.color = "green";
    }
}
```

✓ Explanation:

- We get the user's input using
  document.getElementById("nameInput").value.
- If the user doesn't enter anything, we show an error message in **red**.

- If the user enters their name, we greet them with a **green message**.

Step 5: Open the Project in a Browser

1. Open the **index.html** file in your web browser.
2. Enter your name and click the **Submit** button.
3. You should see a personalized greeting message appear! 🎉

21.2 Handling User Input
21.2.1 What is User Input?

User input refers to data that a user enters into a web page, such as typing in a **text box**, selecting from a **dropdown menu**, or clicking a **button**.

21.2.2 Example: Handling Button Clicks

Let's modify our JavaScript to count how many times a button is clicked.

Updated JavaScript (script.js)

```javascript
let count = 0;

function countClicks() {
  count++;
  document.getElementById("message").innerHTML = "You clicked
the button " + count + " times!";
}
```

Updated HTML (index.html)

```html
<button onclick="countClicks()">Click Me!</button>
<p id="message"></p>
```

Expected Output:

- Each time you click the button, the count increases:
  - "You clicked the button **1** time!"
  - "You clicked the button **2** times!"

21.3 Displaying Data Dynamically

Dynamic data means content that **changes** based on user actions.

21.3.1 Example: Showing Live Time

Let's display the **current time** on our webpage.

Updated JavaScript (script.js)

```javascript
function showTime() {
```

```
    let currentTime = new Date().toLocaleTimeString();
    document.getElementById("message").innerHTML = "Current Time:
" + currentTime;
}


// Update time every second
setInterval(showTime, 1000);
```

Updated HTML (index.html)

```
<p id="message"></p>
```

✓ **Now, the page will update every second to show the current time!**

Try these exercises to practice what you've learned!

1. **Modify the web app** to display a **good morning/good evening** message based on the current time.
2. **Add a reset button** to clear the input field and reset the displayed message.
3. **Create a counter** that starts at 10 and decreases each time a button is clicked.

Short Answer Questions – Hour 21

1. What are the three main technologies used in web development?
2. What is the purpose of JavaScript in a web page?
3. How do you create a button in HTML?
4. What does document.getElementById() do?
5. How can you change the text color dynamically using JavaScript?
6. What is an event in JavaScript?
7. How do you write a function in JavaScript?
8. What does setInterval() do?
9. How do you link an external CSS file to an HTML file?
10. What happens when you use innerHTML in JavaScript?

This concludes **Hour 21**!

Hour 22
JavaScript Best Practices

Writing Clean and Maintainable Code, Performance Optimization, and Security Practices

JavaScript is a powerful programming language, but writing **clean, efficient, and secure code** is essential for creating high-quality applications. This hour will guide you through **best practices** that every JavaScript developer should follow.

22.1 Writing Clean and Maintainable Code

Writing clean code means writing JavaScript in a way that is **easy to read, understand, and modify**. This is important because **code is read more often than it is written**.

22.1.1 Use Meaningful Variable and Function Names

Bad variable names can make your code **confusing**. Always use **descriptive names** that indicate the purpose of the variable or function.

✖ **Bad Example:**

```javascript
let x = 10;
let y = 20;
let z = x + y;
console.log(z);
```

✓ **Good Example:**

```javascript
let applePrice = 10;
let bananaPrice = 20;
let totalPrice = applePrice + bananaPrice;
console.log(totalPrice); // Output: 30
```

22.1.2 Use Proper Formatting and Indentation

Code should be properly **formatted and indented** to improve readability.

✖ **Bad Formatting:**

```javascript
function addNumbers(a,b){return a+b;}
```

✓ **Good Formatting:**

```javascript
function addNumbers(a, b) {
  return a + b;
```

```
}
```

22.1.3 Keep Functions Small and Focused

A function should **do one thing and do it well**. If a function is too long,
break it into smaller functions.

❌ **Bad Example (Large function doing multiple tasks):**

```
function processOrder(order) {
  console.log("Processing order...");
  order.status = "processed";
  sendEmail(order.customerEmail);
  updateDatabase(order);
}
```

✓ **Good Example (Breaking into smaller functions):**

```
function processOrder(order) {
  console.log("Processing order...");
  order.status = "processed";
  notifyCustomer(order.customerEmail);
  saveToDatabase(order);
}

function notifyCustomer(email) {
  console.log("Sending email to " + email);
}

function saveToDatabase(order) {
  console.log("Order saved to database.");
}
```

22.1.4 Avoid Repetitive Code (DRY Principle)

DRY (**Don't Repeat Yourself**) means **writing reusable functions** instead
of repeating the same code.

❌ **Bad Example (Repeated Code):**

```
let area1 = 5 * 5;
let area2 = 10 * 10;
console.log(area1);
console.log(area2);
```

✓ **Good Example (Using a Function to Reuse Code):**

```
function calculateArea(side) {
  return side * side;
}
console.log(calculateArea(5)); // Output: 25
console.log(calculateArea(10)); // Output: 100
```

22.2 Performance Optimization Techniques

Optimizing performance helps in **making applications faster and more efficient.**

22.2.1 Use Efficient Loops

Instead of **using slow loops**, use **optimized methods.**

✖ **Bad Example (Slow Loop):**

```
let numbers = [1, 2, 3, 4, 5];
for (let i = 0; i < numbers.length; i++) {
  console.log(numbers[i]);
}
```

✓ **Good Example (Using forEach):**

```
let numbers = [1, 2, 3, 4, 5];
numbers.forEach(number => console.log(number));
```

22.2.2 Avoid Unnecessary Variables

Unnecessary variables **consume memory and slow down the application.**

✖ **Bad Example (Unnecessary Variable):**

```
let temp = 10;
let result = temp * 2;
console.log(result);
```

✓ **Good Example (Direct Calculation):**

```
console.log(10 * 2); // Output: 20
```

22.2.3 Use Asynchronous JavaScript

Asynchronous JavaScript prevents **blocking the main thread** and makes applications faster.

✖ **Bad Example (Synchronous Code Blocking Execution):**

```
function fetchData() {
  let data = fetch("https://api.example.com/data");
```

```
    console.log(data);
}
fetchData();
console.log("Other tasks...");
```

✓ Good Example (Using Async/Await):

```
async function fetchData() {
    let response = await fetch("https://api.example.com/data");
    let data = await response.json();
    console.log(data);
}
fetchData();
console.log("Other tasks...");
```

22.3 Security Best Practices

Security is **important to protect data and users from attacks**.

22.3.1 Avoid Using eval()

Using eval() is dangerous because it can execute malicious code.

✕ Bad Example:

```
let userCode = "console.log('Hacked!')";
eval(userCode); // This can execute any code
```

✓ Good Example:

```
let userInput = "Hacked!";
console.log(userInput); // Safe Output
```

22.3.2 Use const and let Instead of var

Using var can lead to **unintentional bugs**.

✕ Bad Example (var allows redeclaration):

```
var password = "secret";
var password = "newSecret"; // No error, but a security risk
console.log(password);
```

✓ Good Example (let prevents redeclaration):

```
let password = "secret";
// let password = "newSecret"; // This will cause an error
console.log(password);
```

22.3.3 Validate User Inputs

Never trust user inputs. **Always validate them** before processing.

✖ **Bad Example (No Input Validation):**

```
let username = prompt("Enter username:");
console.log("Hello, " + username);
```

✓ **Good Example (Using Input Validation):**

```
let username = prompt("Enter username:");
if (username.match(/^[a-zA-Z0-9]+$/)) {
    console.log("Hello, " + username);
} else {
    console.log("Invalid username!");
}
```

📌 **Summary Table: JavaScript Best Practices**

Category	Bad Practice	Good Practice
Variable Names	let x = 10;	let price = 10;
Loops	for loop	.forEach() method
Security	Using eval()	Avoiding eval()
Code Reusability	Repeating code	Using functions
Asynchronous Calls	Blocking fetch	Using async/await

Exercise 1: Fix the Formatting

Reformat the following code:

```
function calc(a,b){return a+b;}
console.log(calc(5,10));
```

Exercise 2: Optimize the Loop

Rewrite this loop using .forEach():

```
let colors = ["Red", "Blue", "Green"];
for (let i = 0; i < colors.length; i++) {
    console.log(colors[i]);
}
```

Exercise 3: Secure the Input

Validate the user's input to allow only numbers:

```
let userAge = prompt("Enter your age:");
console.log("Your age is: " + userAge);
```

Short Answer Questions

1. Why is using meaningful variable names important?
2. What is the DRY principle?
3. Why should you avoid eval()?
4. What is the difference between var, let, and const?
5. Why is input validation necessary?
6. What is the benefit of using .forEach()?
7. Why should functions be small and focused?
8. How does asynchronous JavaScript improve performance?
9. What is a security risk of using var?
10. How does async/await help in handling API requests?

This completes **Hour 22: JavaScript Best Practices**!

# Hour 23
Introduction to Node.js

23.1 What is Node.js?
23.1.1 Understanding Node.js in Simple Terms

JavaScript was originally designed to run only in web browsers. But what if we want to run JavaScript **outside the browser**—on a computer or a server? This is where **Node.js** comes in.

Node.js is a runtime environment that allows JavaScript to run on the server-side (outside the browser). It is built on **Google Chrome's V8 JavaScript Engine**, which makes it **fast and efficient**.

23.1.2 Why Use Node.js?

- **Run JavaScript Everywhere** – You can use the same JavaScript code for both the browser and the backend.
- **Fast and Lightweight** – Node.js uses **non-blocking I/O**, making it great for handling multiple requests at once.
- **Built-in Modules** – Node.js provides many built-in modules like **fs (file system), http, path**, etc.
- **Community Support** – It has a large ecosystem with thousands of ready-to-use packages via **npm (Node Package Manager).**

23.1.3 Installing Node.js

Before using Node.js, we need to install it.

Step 1: Download and Install Node.js

1. Go to **https://nodejs.org**
2. Download the latest **LTS (Long-Term Support)** version for your system (Windows, Mac, or Linux).
3. Install it like any other software.

Step 2: Check Installation

After installation, open **Command Prompt (Windows) or Terminal (Mac/Linux)** and type:

```
node -v
```

Output:

v18.14.0 (Version may differ)
To check if **npm** is installed, type:

npm -v

Output:

9.6.1 (Version may differ)

23.2 Running JavaScript on the Server
23.2.1 Running Your First Node.js Program

Unlike traditional JavaScript that runs in a browser, in Node.js, we run JavaScript files using the **command line**.

Step 1: Create a JavaScript File

1. Open **VS Code** or any text editor.
2. Create a file named server.js.
3. Add the following code:

console.log("Hello from Node.js!");

Step 2: Run the File

In the terminal, navigate to the folder where server.js is saved and run:
node server.js

Output:

Hello from Node.js!
Now, you have successfully executed JavaScript **outside the browser** using Node.js.

23.2.2 Creating a Simple HTTP Server

Node.js can be used to create a basic web server without installing anything extra.

Example: Creating a Web Server

Create a new file named **app.js** and add this code:

```javascript
const http = require('http');

const server = http.createServer((req, res) => {
  res.writeHead(200, {'Content-Type': 'text/plain'});
  res.end('Hello, this is my first Node.js server!');
});

server.listen(3000, () => {
  console.log('Server is running at http://localhost:3000');
});
```

Step 1: Run the Server

node app.js

Step 2: Open Browser and Visit

Go to http://localhost:3000 and you will see:
Hello, this is my first Node.js server!
This is how easy it is to create a basic web server using Node.js.

23.3 Basic File System Operations in Node.js

The **fs (file system) module** in Node.js allows us to work with files.

23.3.1 Writing to a File

Let's create a file and write some content into it.

```
const fs = require('fs');

fs.writeFile('myfile.txt', 'Hello, this is written using Node.js!', (err) => {
    if (err) throw err;
    console.log('File has been created and text written!');
});
```

Output:

```
File has been created and text written!
Check the folder where the script is saved, and you will see a
new file myfile.txt with the written content.
```

23.3.2 Reading from a File

We can read the content of a file using fs.readFile().

```
fs.readFile('myfile.txt', 'utf8', (err, data) => {
    if (err) throw err;
    console.log('File Content:', data);
});
```

Output:

```
File Content: Hello, this is written using Node.js!
```

23.3.3 Appending Data to a File

To add more content to an existing file, use fs.appendFile().

```
fs.appendFile('myfile.txt', '\nThis is new content appended.', (err) => {
    if (err) throw err;
```

```
    console.log('New content added!');
});
```

Output:

```
New content added!
```

Now, when you open **myfile.txt**, you will see the additional text.

23.3.4 Deleting a File

If you no longer need a file, you can delete it using fs.unlink().

```
fs.unlink('myfile.txt', (err) => {
    if (err) throw err;
    console.log('File deleted successfully!');
});
```

Output:

```
File deleted successfully!
```

Use Cases of Node.js

Use Case	Description
Web Servers	Build fast, scalable web applications.
APIs	Create RESTful APIs for mobile apps and web apps.
File Management	Read, write, and manage files efficiently.
Real-time Apps	Used for chat applications, gaming, and live updates.
Internet of Things (IoT)	Used in devices like smart home automation.

Practical Exercises

1. Write a Node.js program that creates a new file and writes "Learning Node.js is fun!" into it.
2. Modify the previous program to read the content of the file and display it in the console.
3. Create a basic Node.js web server that responds with "Welcome to my website!" when visited.

Short Answer Questions

1. What is Node.js?
2. Why is Node.js useful for web development?
3. How do you install Node.js on your computer?
4. How can you check the installed Node.js version?
5. What command is used to run a JavaScript file in Node.js?
6. What is the http module used for?
7. Write a simple command to create a file using Node.js.
8. How do you delete a file using Node.js?
9. What does fs.readFile() do?
10. Mention two real-world use cases of Node.js.

This **Hour 23** explanation ensures **complete beginners** can learn **Node.js from scratch** with simple language, **step-by-step examples, outputs, assignments, and use cases**.

Hour 24
Final Project
A Complete JavaScript Web App

Creating an Interactive To-Do List

24.1 Introduction to the Final Project

By now, you have learned all the fundamental concepts of JavaScript. It's time to bring everything together by building a **simple yet functional To-Do List Web App**. This app will allow users to **add, delete, and mark tasks as complete**. We will also store tasks in the browser using **Local Storage**, so they remain even after refreshing the page.

24.2 Features of the To-Do List App

Before diving into coding, let's break down what our app will do:

- ☑ Users can add tasks to a list.
- ☑ Users can remove tasks if they are no longer needed.
- ☑ Users can mark tasks as "completed."
- ☑ Tasks will be saved using **Local Storage**, so they won't disappear after page refresh.

24.3 Setting Up the Project

Before writing JavaScript, let's create the basic **HTML and CSS** structure.

24.3.1 Project Files

Create a folder named ToDoApp, then create the following files inside it:
- index.html → Contains the structure of the app.
- style.css → Handles the styling of the app.
- script.js → Contains JavaScript logic.

24.4 Writing the HTML Structure

Create a simple **index.html** file:

```html
<!DOCTYPE html>
<html lang="en">
<head>
  <meta charset="UTF-8">
  <meta name="viewport" content="width=device-width, initial-scale=1.0">
  <title>To-Do List App</title>
  <link rel="stylesheet" href="style.css">
```

```html
</head>
<body>
  <div class="container">
    <h1>To-Do List</h1>
    <input type="text" id="taskInput" placeholder="Enter a new task">
    <button onclick="addTask()">Add Task</button>
    <ul id="taskList"></ul>
  </div>
  <script src="script.js"></script>
</body>
</html>
```

Explanation of Code

- We create a div with the class **container** to hold the entire app.
- An **input field** allows users to enter tasks.
- A **button** calls the addTask() function when clicked.
- An empty **unordered list (<ul>)** will store tasks dynamically.

24.5 Styling the App with CSS

Create a **style.css** file to improve the appearance:

```css
body {
   font-family: Arial, sans-serif;
   background-color: #f4f4f4;
   text-align: center;
}

.container {
   width: 300px;
   margin: 50px auto;
   background: white;
   padding: 20px;
   box-shadow: 0px 0px 10px gray;
   border-radius: 5px;
}

input {
   width: 80%;
   padding: 5px;
}
```

```css
button {
  padding: 5px 10px;
  background: blue;
  color: white;
  border: none;
  cursor: pointer;
}

ul {
  list-style: none;
  padding: 0;
}

li {
  padding: 10px;
  border-bottom: 1px solid #ddd;
}

.completed {
  text-decoration: line-through;
  color: gray;
}
```

24.6 Writing JavaScript Logic

Create a **script.js** file and add the following JavaScript:

```javascript
document.addEventListener("DOMContentLoaded", loadTasks);

function addTask() {
  let taskInput = document.getElementById("taskInput");
  let taskText = taskInput.value.trim();

  if (taskText === "") {
    alert("Task cannot be empty!");
    return;
  }

  let taskList = document.getElementById("taskList");
  let li = document.createElement("li");
  li.textContent = taskText;

  li.addEventListener("click", () => {
```

```javascript
      li.classList.toggle("completed");
      saveTasks();
    });

    let deleteBtn = document.createElement("button");
    deleteBtn.textContent = "X";
    deleteBtn.style.marginLeft = "10px";
    deleteBtn.onclick = () => {
      taskList.removeChild(li);
      saveTasks();
    };

    li.appendChild(deleteBtn);
    taskList.appendChild(li);

    saveTasks();
    taskInput.value = "";
}

function saveTasks() {
    let tasks = [];
    document.querySelectorAll("#taskList li").forEach(li => {
      tasks.push({ text: li.textContent.replace("X", "").trim(), completed:
li.classList.contains("completed") });
    });
    localStorage.setItem("tasks", JSON.stringify(tasks));
}

function loadTasks() {
    let savedTasks = JSON.parse(localStorage.getItem("tasks")) || [];
    let taskList = document.getElementById("taskList");

    savedTasks.forEach(task => {
      let li = document.createElement("li");
      li.textContent = task.text;

      if (task.completed) {
        li.classList.add("completed");
      }

      li.addEventListener("click", () => {
```

```javascript
      li.classList.toggle("completed");
      saveTasks();
    });

    let deleteBtn = document.createElement("button");
    deleteBtn.textContent = "X";
    deleteBtn.style.marginLeft = "10px";
    deleteBtn.onclick = () => {
      taskList.removeChild(li);
      saveTasks();
    };

    li.appendChild(deleteBtn);
    taskList.appendChild(li);
  });
}
```

Explanation of Code

- **addTask()**: Adds a new task to the list and saves it to Local Storage.
- **saveTasks()**: Stores tasks in the browser to keep them after refresh.
- **loadTasks()**: Loads saved tasks from Local Storage when the page loads.
- **Clicking a task** toggles the **"completed"** class.
- **Clicking the "X" button** deletes the task.

24.7 Running and Testing the App

1. Open the index.html file in a web browser.
2. Add tasks using the input field.
3. Click on a task to mark it as completed.
4. Click "X" to delete a task.
5. Refresh the page – the tasks should **remain** thanks to Local Storage!

24.8 Use Cases of a To-Do App

- **Students** can track their homework.
- **Office workers** can manage daily tasks.
- **Freelancers** can list project deadlines.

Complete the following tasks:

1. Modify the app to **edit a task** when double-clicked.
2. Add a **"Clear All"** button to remove all tasks at once.
3. Customize the app by adding **colors, fonts, or animations**.

Short Answer Questions

1. What is Local Storage in JavaScript?
2. How does addEventListener() work?
3. What is the difference between .classList.add() and .classList.toggle()?
4. How does JSON.stringify() help in saving data?
5. Why do we use DOMContentLoaded in JavaScript?
6. What happens when you call taskList.removeChild(li)?
7. What does querySelectorAll() do?
8. How can you prevent an empty task from being added?
9. What are the advantages of using JavaScript for front-end development?
10. How can you enhance this To-Do app further?

This concludes **Hour 24**! You have now built a fully functional JavaScript web app!

Appendix A
JavaScript Cheat Sheet

A Quick Reference Guide for Beginners

This **JavaScript Cheat Sheet** will serve as a **quick reference** for all the essential JavaScript concepts. It is structured in a **beginner-friendly** manner with **detailed explanations, practical examples, outputs, use cases, and tables for extra properties**.

A.1 JavaScript Basics
A.1.1 What is JavaScript?

- **Definition**

JavaScript is a **programming language** that makes websites **interactive**. It allows us to add **dynamic behavior** to web pages, such as clicking a button, changing colors, updating text, and more.

- **Why JavaScript?**
  JavaScript is used because:
  - ☑ It runs in **web browsers** without additional installation.
  - ☑ It is used to create **dynamic and interactive** web pages.
  - ☑ It can **control HTML & CSS**, modify content, and create animations.
- **Example: First JavaScript Program**

Let's write our **first JavaScript program**.
Example: Display "Hello, World!" on the web page.

```html
<!DOCTYPE html>
<html lang="en">
<head>
  <title>My First JavaScript</title>
</head>
<body>
<h1>Welcome to JavaScript!</h1>
<p id="message"></p>
<script>
  document.getElementById("message").innerHTML = "Hello, World!";
</script>

</body>
```

```
</html>
```

Output:

```
Hello, World! (Displayed inside the webpage)
```

Use Case: Where is JavaScript Used?

- **Web Development** – To create dynamic web pages.
- **Games Development** – JavaScript is used for browser-based games.
- **Server-Side Development** – Using **Node.js**, JavaScript runs on servers.

A.1.2 JavaScript Syntax & Writing Code

JavaScript follows a simple **syntax (rules for writing code)**.

1. How to Write JavaScript?

There are three ways to add JavaScript to a web page:

Method	Example	Use Case
Inline JavaScript	`<button onclick="alert('Hello!')">Click Me</button>`	Used for small scripts
Internal JavaScript	`<script> alert("Welcome!"); </script>`	Used inside an HTML file
External JavaScript	`<script src="script.js"></script>`	Recommended for large projects

2. JavaScript is Case-Sensitive

JavaScript treats **uppercase and lowercase** differently.

☑ **Correct:**

```
let name = "Alice";
console.log(name); // Alice
```

🚫 **Incorrect:**

```
let name = "Alice";
console.log(Name); // Error: Name is not defined
```

3. JavaScript Statements & Semicolons

- JavaScript code consists of **statements**.
- Each statement should end with a **semicolon (;)** *(optional but recommended for better readability)*.

144

Example:

```
let a = 5;
let b = 10;
let sum = a + b;
console.log(sum);  // Output: 15
```

A.2 JavaScript Variables and Data Types
A.2.1 JavaScript Variables

- **What is a Variable?**

A **variable** is a container that **stores values**. It can hold numbers, text, or other data.

- **Declaring Variables**

JavaScript provides **three ways** to declare variables:

Keyword	Use Case	Example
var	Old way, can be redeclared	var age = 25;
let	Modern way, block-scoped	let name = "John";
const	Cannot be changed	const PI = 3.14;

- **Example: Using Variables**

```
let name = "Alice";
let age = 25;
const country = "India";
console.log(name, age, country);
```

Output:

```
Alice 25 India
```

Use Case: Why Variables?
- Used to **store user input** (e.g., form data).
- Helps **manipulate and update** values dynamically.
- Makes code **reusable** and **easy to modify**.

A.3 JavaScript Operators
A.3.1 Arithmetic Operators

Operators are used to **perform calculations** in JavaScript.

Operator	Description	Example	Output
+	Addition	5 + 3	8

Operator	Description	Example	Output
-	Subtraction	10 - 4	6
*	Multiplication	3 * 2	6
/	Division	10 / 2	5

Example:

```
let num1 = 10;
let num2 = 5;
console.log(num1 + num2); // Output: 15
```

Use Case: Where are Operators Used?
- **Calculating total price in shopping carts.**
- **Checking conditions in a game (e.g., score calculation).**

Try these practical exercises to strengthen your understanding!

A.1 Assignment

1. Write a JavaScript program that displays "Welcome to JavaScript Learning!" inside a webpage.
2. Declare three variables (name, age, city) and print them using console.log().
3. Perform a simple calculation: Add **25** and **10**, and display the result.

Short Answer Questions (Appendix A)

Test your knowledge with these questions:
1. What is JavaScript?
2. How does JavaScript make web pages interactive?
3. What are the three ways to write JavaScript?
4. What is the difference between var, let, and const?
5. Why is JavaScript case-sensitive?
6. What is an operator in JavaScript?
7. How do you store values in JavaScript?
8. What is the purpose of semicolons in JavaScript?
9. Write a simple JavaScript program that multiplies two numbers.
10. What is an example of a real-life use case for JavaScript?

Appendix B
Common JavaScript Errors
How to Fix Them

Welcome to **Appendix B**, where we will explore common JavaScript errors and learn how to fix them. JavaScript, like any programming language, has rules that must be followed. If you break these rules, the computer won't understand what you're asking it to do, and it will show an error.

Don't worry! Errors are a normal part of coding, and the key to mastering JavaScript is **understanding why errors happen and how to fix them**. In this appendix, we will go through the most common JavaScript errors with **easy explanations, multiple examples, outputs, use cases, and solutions**.

B.1: Understanding JavaScript Errors

Before we dive into specific errors, let's first understand **what an error is** and how JavaScript informs us about errors.

B.1.1: What is an Error in JavaScript?

An **error** in JavaScript occurs when the browser **cannot understand or execute** a command due to incorrect syntax or logic. Errors can happen for many reasons, such as:

- **Spelling mistakes** in function names or variables.
- **Forgetting to close brackets {} or ()**.
- **Using variables that don't exist**.
- **Performing an operation that is not allowed** (e.g., dividing by zero).

When an error occurs, JavaScript **displays a message** in the console, helping you understand the problem.

Example: Seeing an Error in the Console

```
console.log(Hello World);
```

Output:

```
Uncaught SyntaxError: Unexpected identifier 'World'
```

What went wrong?
- We forgot to **use quotes (" ")** around the text.
- JavaScript **thinks** Hello is a variable, but it is not defined.

Corrected Code:

```
console.log("Hello World");
```

Correct Output:

```
Hello World
```

> ☑ **Fix:** Always wrap text in quotes (" " or ' ').

B.2: Common JavaScript Errors

B.2.1: SyntaxError – Missing or Unexpected Tokens

A **SyntaxError** occurs when JavaScript does not understand the command due to missing symbols like brackets, semicolons, or incorrect usage of keywords.

Example 1: Missing Parentheses in Function Call

```
function greet {
   console.log("Hello!");
}

greet();
```

Output:

```
Uncaught SyntaxError: Unexpected token '{'
```

What went wrong?

- The function **greet** is missing **parentheses ()** in its definition.

Corrected Code:

```
function greet() {
   console.log("Hello!");
}

greet();
```

Correct Output:

```
Hello!
```

> ☑ **Fix:** Always check for missing parentheses when defining functions.

B.2.2: ReferenceError – Using Undefined Variables

A **ReferenceError** occurs when JavaScript tries to use a variable that **has not been declared**.

Example 1: Using an Undeclared Variable

```
console.log(age);
```

Output:

```
Uncaught ReferenceError: age is not defined
```

What went wrong?
- The variable age was **never declared**, but we tried to use it.

Corrected Code:

```
let age = 25;
console.log(age);
```

Correct Output:

```
25
```

☑ **Fix:** Always declare variables with let, const, or var before using them.

B.2.3: TypeError – Calling a Non-Function

A **TypeError** happens when you try to use a value in a way that is not allowed.

Example 1: Trying to Call a String as a Function

```
let message = "Hello";
message();
```

Output:

```
Uncaught TypeError: message is not a function
```

What went wrong?
- message is a **string**, not a function.
- JavaScript **cannot execute a string** like a function.

Corrected Code:

```
let message = "Hello";
console.log(message);
```

Correct Output:

```
Hello
```

> ☑ **Fix:** Ensure that only functions are called with ().

B.3: Table of Common JavaScript Errors

Error Type	Reason	Example	Fix
SyntaxError	Incorrect code structure	console.log("Hello)	Add missing quotes ("Hello").
ReferenceError	Using undefined variables	console.log(name);	Declare variable (let name = "John";).
TypeError	Using values in the wrong way	"text"();	Do not call a non-function as a function.

B.4: Use Cases of Fixing JavaScript Errors
Use Case 1: Debugging a Login System

A developer is building a login system and gets an error:

```
function checkLogin() {
  let username = prompt("Enter username:");
  if username === "admin" { // ERROR HERE
    console.log("Welcome!");
  }
}
```

Error Output:

```
Uncaught SyntaxError: Unexpected identifier 'username'
```

Fix: Add parentheses around if condition.

```
function checkLogin() {
  let username = prompt("Enter username:");
  if (username === "admin") {
    console.log("Welcome!");
  }
}
```

Assignment – Fixing Errors in JavaScript
(Appendix B)

Practical Exercises

1. Fix the following code to display "Hello, John" in the console:

```
let name = "John"
console.log(Hello, name);
```

2. Correct the missing function syntax in the code below:

```
function greet
   console.log("Hello!");
}
greet();
```

3. Identify and fix the error in this code:

```
let number = 10;
if number > 5 {
   console.log("Big number!");
}
```

Short Answer Questions

1. What is a JavaScript error?
2. What causes a **SyntaxError**?
3. How do you fix a **ReferenceError**?
4. What is a **TypeError** in JavaScript?
5. Why does console.log(Hello World); give an error?
6. What should always be wrapped in quotes in JavaScript?
7. How can you debug errors in JavaScript?
8. What happens if you try to call a number as a function?
9. Why is it important to declare variables before using them?
10. What is the best way to prevent JavaScript errors?

Assignment Solutions

Assignment Solutions - Practical Exercises

1. Write a JavaScript program to display "Welcome to JavaScript!" in the browser console.

Solution:

```
console.log("Welcome to JavaScript!");
```

Output:

```
Welcome to JavaScript!
```

Explanation:

- The console.log() function is used to print messages in the browser's developer console.
- This message will appear when you open the browser's **Console (F12 → Console tab)**.

2. Write a program to add two numbers and print the result in the console.

Solution:

```
let num1 = 10;
let num2 = 5;
let sum = num1 + num2;
console.log("The sum is:", sum);
```

Output:

```
The sum is: 15
```

Explanation:

- num1 and num2 are declared and assigned values.
- The + operator adds the numbers.
- console.log() prints the result.

3. Create an HTML page with a button that, when clicked, shows an alert message "Button Clicked!".

Solution:

HTML Code (index.html):

```
<!DOCTYPE html>
```

```html
<html lang="en">
<head>
  <title>Button Click Example</title>
</head>
<body>
  <button onclick="showMessage()">Click Me</button>

  <script>
    function showMessage() {
      alert("Button Clicked!");
    }
  </script>
</body>
</html>
```

Explanation:

- The <button> element is given an onclick attribute that calls the showMessage() function.
- The alert() function displays a pop-up message when the button is clicked.

Short Answer Questions and Explanations

1. What is JavaScript?
Answer:

JavaScript is a **programming language** used to make web pages **interactive**. It allows developers to add dynamic content like animations, form validations, and interactive buttons.

---

2. How does JavaScript make web pages interactive?
Answer:

JavaScript makes web pages interactive by:

- Changing HTML content dynamically (document.getElementById("id").innerHTML = "new text";).
- Responding to user actions like **clicks, mouse movements, and keyboard inputs**.
- Validating form inputs before submission.
- Animating elements and updating styles.

---

3. What are the three main components of a web page?
Answer:

1. **HTML (HyperText Markup Language)** – Defines the structure of the webpage.
2. **CSS (Cascading Style Sheets)** – Styles the webpage, including colors, fonts, and layouts.
3. **JavaScript** – Adds interactivity and dynamic features.

---

4. Name two web browsers that support JavaScript.
Answer:
1. **Google Chrome**
2. **Mozilla Firefox**
   (All modern web browsers support JavaScript, including Safari, Edge, and Opera.)

---

5. What is the role of the JavaScript console?
Answer:
The JavaScript console is a debugging tool used to:
- Display messages using console.log().
- Show errors and warnings in scripts.
- Execute JavaScript commands in real time.

To open the console, press **F12** (or **Ctrl + Shift + J** in Chrome).

---

6. How do you display a message in the console?
Answer:
You can use console.log() to display a message in the console:
console.log("Hello, JavaScript!");
Output:
Hello, JavaScript!

---

7. What is the output of console.log("Hello, World!");?
Answer:
Output:
Hello, World!
The string "Hello, World!" is printed in the console.

---

8. Why is JavaScript called an interpreted language?
Answer:
JavaScript is called an **interpreted language** because:
- It is **executed line by line** by the browser without needing compilation.
- The browser **reads and runs** JavaScript instantly.

9. Name two places where JavaScript is used other than web development.

Answer:

1. **Game Development** – JavaScript is used to create browser-based games using libraries like **Phaser.js**.
2. **Server-side Development** – JavaScript is used on servers with **Node.js** to build backend applications.

---

10. What is the difference between HTML, CSS, and JavaScript?

Feature	HTML	CSS	JavaScript
Purpose	Structure of the webpage	Styles and layout	Interactivity
Example	<h1>Hello</h1>	color: red;	alert("Hi!");
Used For	Defining headings, paragraphs, images, etc.	Styling fonts, colors, spacing, etc.	Making buttons, forms, and animations work

---

Summary of Key Concepts

- **JavaScript** adds **interactivity** to websites.
- **console.log()** prints messages in the console.
- **JavaScript is an interpreted language**, meaning the browser runs it **without compilation**.
- **Web pages consist of HTML, CSS, and JavaScript** for structure, style, and interactivity.
- **JavaScript is widely used beyond web development**, including **game development** and **backend programming**.

Assignment Solutions
Exercise 1: Declare and Print Variables
Problem:
Create a program that declares a let variable for your **name, age, and
country**. Print them using console.log().
Solution:

```
let name = "John Doe";
let age = 25;
let country = "USA";

console.log("Name:", name);
console.log("Age:", age);
console.log("Country:", country);
```

Output:

```
Name: John Doe
Age: 25
Country: USA
```

Explanation:
- let is used to declare variables.
- console.log() is used to print the values.

Exercise 2: Use String and Number Methods
Problem:
Write a program that:
- Declares a number and rounds it to **2 decimal places**.
- Declares a string and **converts it to uppercase**.
Solution:

```
let number = 5.6789;
let roundedNumber = number.toFixed(2);
console.log("Rounded Number:", roundedNumber);

let text = "javascript";
let upperText = text.toUpperCase();
```

```
console.log("Uppercase Text:", upperText);
```

Output:

```
Rounded Number: 5.68
Uppercase Text: JAVASCRIPT
```

Explanation:
- toFixed(2) rounds a number to **2 decimal places**.
- toUpperCase() converts a string to **uppercase**.

Exercise 3: Boolean Logic
Problem:
Create a program that checks if a person is eligible to drive (**Age ≥ 18**). Print true or false.
Solution:

```
let age = 20;
let canDrive = age >= 18;
console.log("Eligible to drive:", canDrive);
```

Output:

```
Eligible to drive: true
```

Explanation:
- The condition age >= 18 **checks if the person is 18 or older**.
- The result (true or false) is stored in the canDrive variable.

Short Answer Questions and Solutions

1. What is a variable in JavaScript?
A **variable** is a container that stores a value. Variables allow us to store, update, and manipulate data in JavaScript.
Example:

```
let myName = "Alice";
console.log(myName);
```

Output:

```
Alice
```

2. What are the three ways to declare a variable?

- **var** → Old way (not recommended)
- **let** → Block-scoped, can be reassigned
- **const** → Block-scoped, cannot be reassigned

Example:

```
var x = 5;   // Using var
let y = 10;  // Using let
const z = 15; // Using const
```

---

3. What is the difference between let and const?

Feature	let	const
Can be reassigned?	✅ Yes	❌ No
Can be redeclared?	❌ No	❌ No
Scope	Block-scoped	Block-scoped

Example:

```
let age = 30;
age = 31;  // ✅ Allowed
```

```
const pi = 3.14;
pi = 3.14159;  // ❌ Error! Cannot reassign a constant
```

---

4. What are the main data types in JavaScript?

1. **String** → "Hello"
2. **Number** → 42, 3.14
3. **Boolean** → true, false
4. **Undefined** → A variable without a value
5. **Null** → Represents an empty value
6. **Object** → {name: "Alice", age: 25}
7. **Array** → ["Apple", "Banana"]

Example:

```
let str = "Hello"; // String
let num = 42;      // Number
let isCool = true; // Boolean
```

---

5. How do you check the length of a string?

Use the .length property.

Example:

```
let message = "JavaScript";
console.log(message.length);
```

Output:

```
10
```

6. What is the purpose of console.log()?

console.log() is used to print messages to the browser's console. It helps in debugging.
Example:

```
console.log("Hello, World!");
```

Output:

```
Hello, World!
```

7. How do you write a single-line comment in JavaScript?

Use // before the comment.
Example:

```
// This is a comment
console.log("Hello");
```

8. What are Boolean values?

Boolean values represent **true or false**.
Example:

```
let isAdult = 18 > 16;
console.log(isAdult);
```

Output:

```
true
```

9. What is the difference between undefined and null?

Feature	undefined	null
Default value?	☑ Yes	✕ No
Meaning	Variable has no value	Empty value

Example:

```javascript
let x;
console.log(x); // undefined

let y = null;
console.log(y); // null
```

10. How do you concatenate two strings in JavaScript?

Use the + operator or template literals.

Example 1: Using +

```javascript
let firstName = "John";
let lastName = "Doe";
console.log(firstName + " " + lastName);
```

Output:

```
John Doe
```

Example 2: Using Template Literals

```javascript
let firstName = "John";
let lastName = "Doe";
console.log(`${firstName} ${lastName}`);
```

Output:

```
John Doe
```

Summary of Key Concepts

- **Variables** store values and can be declared using let, const, or var.
- **Data Types** include Strings, Numbers, Booleans, Undefined, Null, Objects, and Arrays.
- **Operators** like +, .length, and .toUpperCase() manipulate strings and numbers.
- **Boolean logic** helps in decision-making using conditions.
- **console.log()** is used for debugging.

Practical Exercises and Solutions

1. Write a program that takes two numbers and prints their sum, difference, product, and quotient.

Solution:

```
let num1 = 10;
let num2 = 5;

console.log("Sum:", num1 + num2);
console.log("Difference:", num1 - num2);
console.log("Product:", num1 * num2);
console.log("Quotient:", num1 / num2);
```

Output:

```
Sum: 15
Difference: 5
Product: 50
Quotient: 2
```

Explanation:

- The program takes two numbers (num1 and num2).
- It performs arithmetic operations: addition (+), subtraction (-), multiplication (*), and division (/).
- The results are displayed using console.log().

2. Create a JavaScript program that checks whether a user is eligible for a senior citizen discount (age 60 or above).

Solution:

```
let age = 65; // Example age

if (age >= 60) {
   console.log("You are eligible for a senior citizen discount.");
} else {
   console.log("You are not eligible for a senior citizen discount.");
}
```

Output:

You are eligible for a senior citizen discount.

Explanation:

- The program checks if the age is **60 or more**.
- If age >= 60, it prints eligibility for the discount.
- Otherwise, it prints that the user is **not eligible**.

---

3. Write a program that asks the user for a number and checks if it is even or odd.

Solution:

```javascript
let number = 7; // Example number

if (number % 2 === 0) {
   console.log(number + " is even.");
} else {
   console.log(number + " is odd.");
}
```

Output:

```
7 is odd.
```

Explanation:

- The modulus operator (%) is used to check if the remainder is 0.
- If number % 2 === 0, it is **even**, otherwise, it is **odd**.

Short Answer Questions and Explanations

1. What is an operator in JavaScript?

An **operator** is a symbol used to perform operations on values. JavaScript has different types of operators, such as:

- **Arithmetic Operators** (+, -, *, /, %)
- **Comparison Operators** (==, ===, >, <, >=, <=)
- **Logical Operators** (&&, ||, !)
- **Assignment Operators** (=, +=, -=, *=, /=)

---

2. What is the difference between == and ===?

Operator	Name	Comparison Type	Example
==	Loose Equality	Compares values, but ignores type	5 == "5" → true

Operator	Name	Comparison Type	Example
===	Strict Equality	Compares values **and** types	5 === "5" → false

3. What does the modulus operator % do?

The modulus (%) operator **returns the remainder** of division.
Example:

console.log(10 % 3); // Output: 1

- 10 / 3 gives a quotient of 3 with a remainder of 1.
- So, 10 % 3 is 1.

4. What are logical operators?

Logical operators are used to perform boolean logic:

- && (**AND**) → Returns true if **both** conditions are true.
- || (**OR**) → Returns true if **at least one** condition is true.
- ! (**NOT**) → Reverses true to false and vice versa.

Example:

```
console.log(true && false); // false
console.log(true || false); // true
console.log(!true); // false
```

5. How do you concatenate strings in JavaScript?

You can concatenate strings using **the + operator** or **template literals (``)**.
Example using +:

```
let name = "John";
let message = "Hello, " + name + "!";
console.log(message);
```

Output:

```
Hello, John!
```

Example using **template literals**:

```
let message = `Hello, ${name}!`;
console.log(message);
```

Output (same as above):

```
Hello, John!
```

6. What is the purpose of parentheses in operator precedence?

Parentheses () **override operator precedence** and ensure correct evaluation order.

Example:

```
let result = (2 + 3) * 4;
console.log(result); // Output: 20
```

Without parentheses:

```
let result = 2 + 3 * 4;
console.log(result); // Output: 14 (Multiplication is done first)
```

---

7. Give an example of a program that uses comparison operators.

Comparison operators compare values and return true or false.

Example:

```
let age = 18;
console.log(age >= 18); // Output: true
```

- >= checks if age is greater than or equal to 18.

---

8. What will be the output of 5 + "5"?

```
console.log(5 + "5");
```

Output:

```
"55"
```

Explanation:
- When a **number** and a **string** are added using +, JavaScript converts the number into a string.
- "5" + "5" results in "55" (string concatenation).

---

9. How do template literals differ from normal string concatenation?

Template literals (``) allow **multi-line strings** and **embedded expressions**.

Example:

```
let name = "Alice";
console.log(`Hello, ${name}! Welcome.`);
```

Output:

```
Hello, Alice! Welcome.
```

- **No need for + operators**
- **Supports variables inside ${}**
- **Supports multi-line strings**

10. What is the difference between && and ||?

Operator	Name	Behavior
&&	Logical AND	Returns true if **both** conditions are true
`		`

Example:

```
console.log(true && false); // false
console.log(true || false); // true
```

Summary of Key Concepts

- **Operators** perform operations on values.
- **Arithmetic Operators** handle mathematical calculations.
- **Comparison Operators** check relationships between values.
- **Logical Operators** (&&, ||, !) evaluate boolean expressions.
- **Template Literals** (``` `` ```) provide better string handling than +.
- **Parentheses** control evaluation order in expressions.

Exercise 1: Temperature Checker
Problem:
Write a JavaScript program that checks the temperature and prints:
- "It's too cold!" if temperature < 10
- "It's warm." if temperature is between 10 and 25
- "It's hot!" if temperature > 25

Solution:

```javascript
function checkTemperature(temp) {
  if (temp < 10) {
    console.log("It's too cold!");
  } else if (temp >= 10 && temp <= 25) {
    console.log("It's warm.");
  } else {
    console.log("It's hot!");
  }
}
// Example Usage
checkTemperature(5);   // Output: It's too cold!
checkTemperature(15);  // Output: It's warm.
checkTemperature(30);  // Output: It's hot!
```

Exercise 2: Leap Year Checker
Problem:
Write a program to check if a given year is a leap year or not.
Solution:

```javascript
function isLeapYear(year) {
  if ((year % 4 === 0 && year % 100 !== 0) || (year % 400 === 0)) {
    console.log(year + " is a leap year.");
  } else {
    console.log(year + " is not a leap year.");
  }
}
// Example Usage
isLeapYear(2024);  // Output: 2024 is a leap year.
isLeapYear(2023);  // Output: 2023 is not a leap year.
isLeapYear(2000);  // Output: 2000 is a leap year.
```

```
isLeapYear(1900);  // Output: 1900 is not a leap year.
```

Explanation:

- A year is a leap year if it is divisible by 4 **and** not divisible by 100 **unless** it is also divisible by 400.

Exercise 3: Password Strength Checker
Problem:
Write a JavaScript program that checks if a password length is:
- "Weak" if less than 6 characters
- "Medium" if between 6 and 10 characters
- "Strong" if more than 10 characters

Solution:

```javascript
function checkPasswordStrength(password) {
  let length = password.length;

  if (length < 6) {
    console.log("Weak");
  } else if (length >= 6 && length <= 10) {
    console.log("Medium");
  } else {
    console.log("Strong");
  }
}
// Example Usage
checkPasswordStrength("abc");     // Output: Weak
checkPasswordStrength("myp@ss12"); // Output: Medium
checkPasswordStrength("SuperSecurePassword123"); //Output: Strong
```

Short Answer Questions and Explanations

1. What is an if-else statement?
An if-else statement is a conditional structure in JavaScript that executes different blocks of code based on a given condition.

Example:

```javascript
let age = 18;
if (age >= 18) {
  console.log("You are an adult.");
```

```
} else {
    console.log("You are a minor.");
}
```

Output:

```
You are an adult.
```

2. What is the difference between if-else and switch case?

Feature	if-else	switch
Usage	Used for **relational** and **logical** conditions (>, <, ==, &&, etc.)	Used for checking **fixed values** (exact matches)
Performance	Slower when there are many conditions	Faster for multiple fixed values
Syntax	More flexible but longer	More concise and readable

Example:
Using if-else:

```
let day = 3;
if (day === 1) console.log("Monday");
else if (day === 2) console.log("Tuesday");
else console.log("Other day");
Using switch:
switch (day) {
    case 1: console.log("Monday"); break;
    case 2: console.log("Tuesday"); break;
    default: console.log("Other day");
}
```

3. What happens if no case matches in a switch statement?

If no case matches, the default case executes (if present).
Example:

```
let fruit = "Mango";
switch (fruit) {
    case "Apple":
        console.log("It's an apple.");
        break;
    case "Banana":
```

```
      console.log("It's a banana.");
      break;
    default:
      console.log("Unknown fruit.");
}
```

Output:

```
Unknown fruit.
```

---

4. Name three falsy values in JavaScript.

Falsy values in JavaScript include:

1. 0
2. "" (empty string)
3. null
4. undefined
5. NaN
6. false

Example:

```
if (0) {
   console.log("Truthy");
} else {
   console.log("Falsy");
}
```

Output:

```
Falsy
```

---

5. What is a truthy value?

Any value that is **not falsy** is truthy.

Examples of truthy values: "Hello", 42, true, [] (empty array), {} (empty object).

Example:

```
if ("Hello") {
   console.log("Truthy");
} else {
   console.log("Falsy");
}
```

Output:

Truthy

6. Why do we use break statements in switch cases?

- break prevents execution from **falling through** to the next case.
- Without break, JavaScript **continues executing all cases below** the matched case.

Example:

```
let color = "red";
switch (color) {
  case "red":
    console.log("Stop!");
  case "yellow":
    console.log("Get Ready!");
  case "green":
    console.log("Go!");
}
```

Output (without break):

```
Stop!
Get Ready!
Go!
```

7. Write an example of an if-else statement.

```
let age = 16;
if (age >= 18) {
  console.log("You can vote.");
} else {
  console.log("You cannot vote yet.");
}
```

Output:

```
You cannot vote yet.
```

8. What is the purpose of an else-if ladder?

- It allows checking **multiple conditions** in a structured way.
- Used when there are **more than two** possible outcomes.

Example:

```javascript
let marks = 85;
if (marks >= 90) {
  console.log("Grade: A");
} else if (marks >= 75) {
  console.log("Grade: B");
} else {
  console.log("Grade: C");
}
```

9. How does JavaScript handle empty strings in conditions?

- An empty string "" is **falsy**.

Example:

```javascript
if ("") {
  console.log("Truthy");
} else {
  console.log("Falsy");
}
```

Output:

```
Falsy
```

10. What will be the output of the following code?

```javascript
if (0) {
  console.log("Truthy");
} else {
  console.log("Falsy");
}
```

Output:

```
Falsy
```

Explanation:

- 0 is a **falsy** value, so the else block executes.

Summary of Key Concepts

- **Conditional statements (if-else, switch)** control the flow of execution.

- **Falsy values (0, "", null, undefined, NaN, false)** cause conditions to fail.
- **Truthy values (any non-falsy value)** cause conditions to pass.
- **break prevents switch cases from falling through.**

Exercise 1: Print Multiplication Table

Problem: Write a program to print the multiplication table of 5 using a for loop.

Solution:

```javascript
for (let i = 1; i <= 10; i++) {
    console.log(`5 x ${i} = ${5 * i}`);
}
```

Output:

```
5 x 1 = 5
5 x 2 = 10
5 x 3 = 15
5 x 4 = 20
5 x 5 = 25
5 x 6 = 30
5 x 7 = 35
5 x 8 = 40
5 x 9 = 45
5 x 10 = 50
```

Explanation:

- **The for loop runs from 1 to 10.**
- **The console.log() statement prints each multiplication step.**

Exercise 2: Sum of Numbers Until User Enters 0

Problem: Write a while loop that asks the user to enter numbers and keeps adding them until the user enters 0. Display the sum.

Solution:

```javascript
let sum = 0;
let number;

while (true) {
  number = parseInt(prompt("Enter a number (0 to stop):"));
  if (number === 0) {
    break;
  }
}
```

```
    sum += number;
}

console.log("Total sum:", sum);
```

Example Input:

```
User enters: 5, 10, 3, 0
```

Output:

```
Total sum: 18
```

Explanation:
- **The loop keeps asking for input until the user enters 0.**
- **The break statement stops the loop when 0 is entered.**

Exercise 3: Reverse a String Using a Loop
Problem: Write a JavaScript program to reverse a string using a loop.
Solution:

```
let str = "JavaScript";
let reversedStr = "";

for (let i = str.length - 1; i >= 0; i--) {
    reversedStr += str[i];
}

console.log("Reversed String:", reversedStr);
```

Output:

```
Reversed String: tpircSavaJ
```

Explanation:
- **The loop starts from the last character and moves to the first.**
- **The reversed string is built character by character.**

Short Answer Questions and Solutions

1. What is a loop in JavaScript?

A loop is a control structure that allows repeating a block of code multiple times until a condition is met.

Example: Printing numbers from 1 to 5 using a loop:

```
for (let i = 1; i <= 5; i++) {
   console.log(i);
}
```

---

2. How does a for loop work?

A for loop runs a block of code a fixed number of times based on a condition.

Example:

```
for (let i = 1; i <= 3; i++) {
   console.log(i);
}
```

Output:

```
1
2
3
```

---

3. What are the three parts of a for loop?

A for loop has three parts:

for (initialization; condition; increment/decrement) {
** // Loop body**
}

- **Initialization: Sets a starting value (let i = 0;).**
- **Condition: The loop runs while this is true (i < 5;).**
- **Increment/Decrement: Updates the variable (i++).**

Example:

```
for (let i = 0; i < 5; i++) {
   console.log(i);
}
```

---

4. How does a while loop differ from a for loop?

- **A for loop is used when the number of iterations is known.**
- **A while loop runs until a condition becomes false.**

Example:

```
let i = 0;
while (i < 5) {
   console.log(i);
   i++;
```

```
    }
```

5. What is the main advantage of a do-while loop?

A do-while loop always runs at least once before checking the condition.

Example:

```
let i = 10;
do {
    console.log(i);
    i++;
} while (i < 5);
```

Output:

```
10
```

Explanation:

Even though i is not less than 5, the loop runs once before checking the condition.

6. What does the break statement do?

The break statement stops a loop immediately when executed.

Example:

```
for (let i = 1; i <= 10; i++) {
    if (i === 5) {
        break;
    }
    console.log(i);
}
```

Output:

```
1
2
3
4
```

The loop stops when i becomes 5.

7. What does the continue statement do?

The continue statement skips the current iteration and moves to the next one.

Example:

```
for (let i = 1; i <= 5; i++) {
  if (i === 3) {
    continue;
  }
  console.log(i);
}
```

Output:

```
1
2
4
5
```

The loop skips 3 but continues running.

---

8. How can you loop through an array using a for loop?

You can use a for loop with the length property to iterate through an array.

Example:

```
let colors = ["Red", "Blue", "Green"];
for (let i = 0; i < colors.length; i++) {
  console.log(colors[i]);
}
```

Output:

```
Red
Blue
Green
```

---

9. How do you use a loop to print characters of a string one by one?

You can use a for loop with charAt() or index notation.

Example:

```
let str = "Hello";
for (let i = 0; i < str.length; i++) {
  console.log(str[i]);
}
```

Output:

```
H
e
```

|
|
o

---

10. Give a real-world example where loops are useful.

Loops are used in automated tasks, like displaying a list of products on a website.

Example: Displaying a list of product names from an array:

```
let products = ["Laptop", "Phone", "Tablet"];
for (let i = 0; i < products.length; i++) {
    console.log("Product:", products[i]);
}
```

Output:

```
Product: Laptop
Product: Phone
Product: Tablet
```

Summary of Key Concepts

- Loops help execute a block of code multiple times.
- for, while, and do-while are the three main types of loops.
- break stops a loop, while continue skips an iteration.
- Loops are commonly used for iterating through arrays and strings.

1. Write a function that takes a number as input and returns its square.
Solution:

```javascript
function square(num) {
  return num * num;
}

console.log(square(5));
```

Output:

```
25
```

Explanation:
- The function square(num) multiplies num by itself and returns the result.
- When we call square(5), it returns 5 * 5 = 25.

2. Create a function that checks if a given number is even or odd.
Solution:

```javascript
function checkEvenOdd(num) {
  if (num % 2 === 0) {
    return "Even";
  } else {
    return "Odd";
  }
}

console.log(checkEvenOdd(7));
console.log(checkEvenOdd(10));
```

Output:

```
Odd
Even
```

Explanation:
- The function checkEvenOdd(num) checks if num % 2 === 0.
- If true, the function returns "Even"; otherwise, it returns "Odd".

3. Write a function that takes two numbers and returns the larger of the two.
Solution:

```javascript
function findMax(a, b) {
   return a > b ? a : b;
}


console.log(findMax(8, 12));
console.log(findMax(15, 5));
```

Output:

```
12
15
```

Explanation:
- The function findMax(a, b) compares a and b.
- The **ternary operator (? :)** returns a if a > b, otherwise it returns b.

<hr>

Short Answer Questions & Solutions

1. What is a function in JavaScript?
A function in JavaScript is a **block of reusable code** that performs a specific task. Functions help organize and structure code efficiently.
Example:

```javascript
function greet() {
   console.log("Hello, World!");
}
greet(); // Calls the function
```

2. How do you define and call a function?
A function is defined using the function keyword, followed by the function name and parentheses ().
Syntax:

```javascript
function functionName() {
   // Code to execute
}
To call a function, use:
functionName();
```

Example:

```
function sayHello() {
   console.log("Hello!");
}
sayHello();
```

Output:

```
Hello!
```

---

3. What are function parameters?

Function parameters are variables that accept values when a function is called.

Example:

```
function greet(name) {
   console.log("Hello, " + name + "!");
}
greet("John");
```

Output:

```
Hello, John!
```

Explanation:

- name is a **parameter** that receives "John" as an **argument**.

---

4. What does the return statement do in a function?

The return statement **sends a value back** from the function.

Example:

```
function add(a, b) {
   return a + b;
}
let sum = add(5, 3);
console.log(sum);
```

Output:

```
8
```

Explanation:

- return a + b; sends the result back to the calling code.

5. Explain the difference between function declaration and function expression.

Type	Definition	Hoisting
Function Declaration	Uses the function keyword and a name.	**Hoisted** (can be used before declaration)
Function Expression	Stored in a variable using const or let.	**Not hoisted** (must be declared first)

Example of **Function Declaration:**

```
function greet() {
   console.log("Hello!");
}
greet(); // Works before or after definition
Example of Function Expression:
const greet = function() {
   console.log("Hello!");
};
greet();
```

6. What is a global variable?

A global variable is declared outside any function and can be used anywhere in the program.

Example:

```
let globalVar = "I am global";

function display() {
   console.log(globalVar);
}
display();
```

Output:

```
I am global
```

7. What is a local variable?

A local variable is **declared inside a function** and can only be used within that function.

Example:

```
function myFunction() {
```

```javascript
    let localVar = "I am local";
    console.log(localVar);
}
myFunction();
// console.log(localVar); // ERROR: localVar is not defined
```

---

8. What is the difference between var, let, and const in terms of scope?

Keyword	Scope	Reassignment	Redeclaration	Hoisting
var	Function-scoped	Yes	Yes	Hoisted with undefined
let	Block-scoped	Yes	No	Hoisted but not initialized
const	Block-scoped	No	No	Hoisted but not initialized

Example:

```javascript
var x = 10; // Can be redeclared
let y = 20; // Cannot be redeclared
const z = 30; // Cannot be reassigned
```

---

9. What is function hoisting?

Function **hoisting** allows function declarations to be used **before they are defined**.

Example:

```javascript
hello();

function hello() {
    console.log("Hello, world!");
}
```

Output:

```
Hello, world!
```

However, function expressions are **not hoisted**:

```javascript
hello(); // ERROR

const hello = function() {
    console.log("Hi!");
```

```
};
```

10. Write an example of a function that returns a string.

Example:

```
function getMessage() {
    return "Welcome to JavaScript!";
}

let message = getMessage();
console.log(message);
```

Output:

```
Welcome to JavaScript!
```

Summary of Key Concepts

- **Functions** are reusable blocks of code.
- **Function parameters** allow us to pass values to functions.
- **The return statement** sends a value back to the calling code.
- **Function declarations are hoisted**, but function expressions are not.
- **Global variables** can be accessed anywhere, while **local variables** are function-specific.
- **var vs. let vs. const**: var is function-scoped, let and const are block-scoped.
- **Hoisting** allows function declarations to be called before they are defined.

1. Create an Object
Task:

- Create an object book with properties: title, author, and yearPublished.
- Access and print author using both **dot notation** and **bracket notation**.

Solution:

```
// Creating the object
let book = {
   title: "The JavaScript Guide",
   author: "John Doe",
   yearPublished: 2021
};

// Accessing author using dot notation
console.log(book.author);

// Accessing author using bracket notation
console.log(book["author"]);
```

Output:

```
John Doe
John Doe
```

Explanation:

- **Dot notation (book.author)** is the most commonly used way to access object properties.
- **Bracket notation (book["author"])** is useful when the property name is dynamic or contains special characters.

2. Modify an Array
Task:

- Create an array colors with three color names.
- Add two colors at the end.
- Remove the first color.
- Print the final array.

Solution:

```javascript
// Creating an array
let colors = ["Red", "Blue", "Green"];

// Adding two colors at the end
colors.push("Yellow", "Purple");

// Removing the first color
colors.shift();

// Printing the final array
console.log(colors);
```

Output:

```
5
'Red'
["Blue", "Green", "Yellow", "Purple"]
```

Explanation:
- **push()** adds elements to the end of an array.
- **shift()** removes the first element of the array.

---

3. Use Object and Array Together
Task:
- Create an array movies with objects inside. Each object should have title, year, and rating.
- Print the name of the first movie.

Solution:
```javascript
// Creating an array of objects
let movies = [
   { title: "Inception", year: 2010, rating: 8.8 },
   { title: "Interstellar", year: 2014, rating: 8.6 },
   { title: "The Dark Knight", year: 2008, rating: 9.0 }
];

// Printing the name of the first movie
console.log(movies[0].title);
```
Output:

```
Inception
```

Explanation:

- Objects inside an array allow us to store multiple structured records.
- movies[0].title accesses the title of the first movie.

Short Answer Questions and Explanations

1. What is an object in JavaScript?

An **object** is a data structure that stores **key-value pairs**. It allows us to store and organize related data together.

Example:

```
let car = { brand: "Toyota", model: "Corolla", year: 2020 };
```

2. How do you access an object's property using dot notation?

You can access a property using a **dot (.) followed by the property name.**

Example:

```
let person = { name: "Alice", age: 30 };
console.log(person.name); // Output: Alice
```

3. How do you add a new property to an object?

You can **add a new property** to an object using **dot notation** or **bracket notation.**

Example:

```
let student = { name: "Bob", age: 20 };
student.grade = "A"; // Adding a new property
console.log(student);
```

Output:

```
{ name: 'Bob', age: 20, grade: 'A' }
```

4. What is the difference between an object and an array?

Feature	Object	Array
Structure	Stores data as key-value pairs	Stores data in an ordered list
Access	Access using property names	Access using index numbers

Feature	Object	Array
Use Case	Good for structured data (e.g., a person)	Good for ordered collections (e.g., a list of numbers)

Example of an **object**:

```
let car = { brand: "Tesla", model: "Model 3" };
```

Example of an **array**:

```
let numbers = [10, 20, 30];
```

5. What does the push() method do in an array?

The **push() method** adds elements to the **end** of an array.

Example:

```
let fruits = ["Apple", "Banana"];
fruits.push("Mango");
console.log(fruits);
```

Output:

```
["Apple", "Banana", "Mango"]
```

6. How do you remove the first element from an array?

Use the **shift() method** to remove the first element.

Example:

```
let colors = ["Red", "Blue", "Green"];
colors.shift();
console.log(colors);
```

Output:

```
["Blue", "Green"]
```

7. What does slice() do in an array?

The **slice(start, end) method** returns a **new array** containing a portion of the original array.

Example:

```
let numbers = [1, 2, 3, 4, 5];
let slicedNumbers = numbers.slice(1, 4);
console.log(slicedNumbers);
```

Output:

```
[2, 3, 4]
```

(The original array remains unchanged.)

8. How do you replace an element in an array?

You can **replace an element** by directly assigning a new value to its index.
Example:

```
let fruits = ["Apple", "Banana", "Mango"];
fruits[1] = "Orange";
console.log(fruits);
```

Output:

```
["Apple", "Orange", "Mango"]
```

9. How do you store multiple student records using objects and arrays?

We can use an **array of objects** to store multiple student records.
Example:

```
let students = [
    { name: "Alice", age: 20 },
    { name: "Bob", age: 22 },
    { name: "Charlie", age: 21 }
];
console.log(students[0].name); // Accessing first student's name
```

Output:

```
Alice
```

10. Explain the use of splice() in arrays.

The **splice(start, deleteCount, item1, item2, …)** method **removes, replaces, or adds elements** in an array.
Example 1: Removing elements

```
let numbers = [1, 2, 3, 4, 5];
numbers.splice(2, 2); // Removes 2 elements starting at index 2
console.log(numbers);
```

Output:

```
[1, 2, 5]
```

Example 2: Adding elements

```
let colors = ["Red", "Blue"];
colors.splice(1, 0, "Green"); // Adds "Green" at index 1
console.log(colors);
```

Output:

```
["Red", "Green", "Blue"]
```

Summary of Key Concepts

- **Objects** store key-value pairs and are useful for structured data.
- **Arrays** store ordered collections of data.
- push() adds elements to an array, while shift() removes the first element.
- slice() extracts parts of an array without modifying the original.
- splice() can add, remove, or replace elements in an array.

1. Write a program that multiplies all numbers in an array by 5 using map().

Solution:

```
let numbers = [1, 2, 3, 4, 5];
let multipliedNumbers = numbers.map(num => num * 5);
console.log(multipliedNumbers);
```

Output:

```
[5, 10, 15, 20, 25]
```

Explanation:

- The map() method creates a **new array** by applying the function (num * 5) to each element.
- It **does not modify** the original array.

2. Write a program that filters out all numbers greater than 50 from an array.

Solution:

```
let numbers = [10, 25, 55, 60, 30, 90, 15];
let filteredNumbers = numbers.filter(num => num <= 50);
console.log(filteredNumbers);
```

Output:

```
[10, 25, 30, 15]
```

Explanation:

- The filter() method **creates a new array** with elements that satisfy the condition (num <= 50).
- The original array remains unchanged.

3. Create an array of prices and use reduce() to calculate the total bill.

Solution:

```
let prices = [100, 200, 50, 150];
let totalBill = prices.reduce((sum, price) => sum + price, 0);
console.log("Total Bill:", totalBill);
```

Output:

```
Total Bill: 500
```

Explanation:
- The reduce() method accumulates values (sum + price).
- The initial value is 0, and each price is added to the total.

✅ Short Answer Questions and Explanations

1. What does the forEach() method do?

The forEach() method **iterates over** an array and executes a function for each element.

Example:

```
let fruits = ["Apple", "Banana", "Mango"];
fruits.forEach(fruit => console.log(fruit));
```

Output:

```
Apple
Banana
Mango
```

Explanation:
- forEach() does not return a new array, it simply **executes a function on each element**.

---

2. How does map() differ from forEach()?

Method	Returns a new array?	Modifies original array?
forEach()	No	No
map()	Yes	No

Example:

```
let nums = [1, 2, 3];
let doubled = nums.map(num => num * 2);
console.log(doubled); // [2, 4, 6]
```

- map() **creates a new array** with modified values, while forEach() does not.

---

3. What is the use of filter() in arrays?

The filter() method **creates a new array** with elements that satisfy a condition.

196

Example:

```
let numbers = [10, 20, 30, 40, 50];
let greaterThan25 = numbers.filter(num => num > 25);
console.log(greaterThan25);
```

Output:

```
[30, 40, 50]
```

4. How do you find the sum of numbers in an array using reduce()?

We use reduce() to **accumulate** values.

Example:

```
let numbers = [5, 10, 15];
let sum = numbers.reduce((total, num) => total + num, 0);
console.log(sum);
```

Output:

```
30
```

5. What does the sort() method do?

The sort() method **sorts elements in place** as **strings by default**.

Example:

```
let numbers = [10, 5, 25, 1];
numbers.sort();
console.log(numbers);
```

Output:

```
[1, 10, 25, 5]
```

Fix for numerical sorting:

```
numbers.sort((a, b) => a - b);
console.log(numbers);
```

Output:

```
[1, 5, 10, 25]
```

6. Can map() modify the original array?

No, map() **does not modify** the original array.

Example:

```
let numbers = [2, 4, 6];
numbers.map(num => num * 2);
console.log(numbers);
```

Output:

```
[2, 4, 6] // Unchanged
```

To store changes:

```
let doubled = numbers.map(num => num * 2);
console.log(doubled);
```

Output:

```
[4, 8, 12]
```

---

7. What are the parameters of forEach()?

The forEach() method takes up to **three** parameters:

1. **Current element**
2. **Index**
3. **Entire array**

Example:

```
let numbers = [10, 20, 30];
numbers.forEach((num, index, array) => {
    console.log(`Value: ${num}, Index: ${index}, Array: ${array}`);
});
```

Output:

```
Value: 10, Index: 0, Array: 10,20,30
Value: 20, Index: 1, Array: 10,20,30
Value: 30, Index: 2, Array: 10,20,30
```

---

8. How can you filter out odd numbers from an array?

Use filter() with a condition:

Example:

```
let numbers = [1, 2, 3, 4, 5];
let evenNumbers = numbers.filter(num => num % 2 === 0);
console.log(evenNumbers);
```

Output:

```
[2, 4]
```

9. What will be the output of ["z", "b", "a"].sort()?

Example:

```javascript
let letters = ["z", "b", "a"];
letters.sort();
console.log(letters);
```

Output:

```
["a", "b", "z"]
```

Explanation:

- sort() arranges elements **alphabetically** by default.

10. What is the initial value in reduce() used for?

The **initial value** is the starting point for accumulation.

Example:

```javascript
let numbers = [10, 20, 30];
let sum = numbers.reduce((total, num) => total + num, 100);
console.log(sum);
```

Output:

```
160
```

Explanation:

- Without 100, it starts from the first element.
- With 100, it starts from 100.

Summary of Key Concepts

- **map()**: Returns a new array after applying a function.
- **filter()**: Returns a new array with elements matching a condition.
- **reduce()**: Reduces an array to a single value.
- **sort()**: Sorts an array alphabetically unless a compare function is used.
- **forEach()**: Loops through an array but does not return a new one.

1. Write a JavaScript program that asks for a user's full name and prints:
- The name in uppercase.
- The name in lowercase.
- The length of the name.

Solution:

```
let fullName = prompt("Enter your full name:");
console.log("Uppercase:", fullName.toUpperCase());
console.log("Lowercase:", fullName.toLowerCase());
console.log("Length:", fullName.length);
```

Example Output:

```
Enter your full name: John Doe
Uppercase: JOHN DOE
Lowercase: john doe
Length: 8
```

Explanation:
- toUpperCase() converts the string to uppercase.
- toLowerCase() converts the string to lowercase.
- .length returns the total number of characters in the string.

2. Create a function that takes a sentence and returns an array of words.
Solution:

```
function getWords(sentence) {
    return sentence.split(" ");
}

console.log(getWords("JavaScript is awesome"));
```

Output:

```
["JavaScript", "is", "awesome"]
```

Explanation:

- The split(" ") method breaks the sentence at spaces and returns an array of words.

3. Write a program that replaces the word "bad" with "good" in a given sentence.

Solution:

```javascript
function replaceBadWithGood(sentence) {
   return sentence.replace("bad", "good");
}

console.log(replaceBadWithGood("This is a bad idea."));
```

Output:

```
"This is a good idea."
```

Explanation:

- replace("bad", "good") searches for "bad" and replaces it with "good".
- It only replaces the **first occurrence** of "bad".

Short Answer Questions and Solutions

1. What is a string in JavaScript?

A **string** is a sequence of characters enclosed in **single (')**, **double (")**, or **backticks (`)**.

Example:

```javascript
let str1 = "Hello"; // Double quotes
let str2 = 'World'; // Single quotes
let str3 = `JavaScript`; // Backticks
```

2. How do you find the length of a string?

You can use the .length property to find the length of a string.

Example:

```javascript
let text = "JavaScript";
console.log(text.length);
```

Output:

```
10
```

3. What is the difference between slice() and split()?

Method	Functionality
slice(start, end)	Extracts a part of a string and returns it.
split(separator)	Splits a string into an array based on a separator.

Example:

```
let text = "Hello World";

// slice
console.log(text.slice(0, 5)); // "Hello"

// split
console.log(text.split(" ")); // ["Hello", "World"]
```

4. How does replace() work in JavaScript?

The replace() method replaces a part of a string with another value.

Example:

```
let sentence = "I love JavaScript!";
console.log(sentence.replace("love", "like"));
```

Output:

```
"I like JavaScript!"
```

Note: It only replaces **the first occurrence** of a word. To replace all occurrences, use a **regular expression**:

```
let text = "bad bad bad";
console.log(text.replace(/bad/g, "good"));
```

Output:

```
"good good good"
```

5. What does trim() do?

The trim() method removes **whitespace** (spaces, newlines, etc.) from the beginning and end of a string.

Example:

```
let name = " John Doe ";
console.log(name.trim());
```

Output:

```
"John Doe"
```

6. What are template literals?

Template literals are strings enclosed in **backticks** (`) that allow **multi-line strings** and **string interpolation (${})**.

Example:

```
let name = "Alice";
console.log(`Hello, my name is ${name}.`);
```

Output:

```
"Hello, my name is Alice."
```

7. How do you convert a string to uppercase?

Use .toUpperCase() to convert a string to uppercase.

Example:

```
let text = "hello";
console.log(text.toUpperCase());
```

Output:

```
"HELLO"
```

8. What is a regular expression?

A **regular expression (RegEx)** is a pattern used to search and manipulate strings.

Example:

```
let sentence = "I love JavaScript!";
let result = /love/.test(sentence);
console.log(result);
```

Output:

```
true
```

9. What is string interpolation?

String interpolation is inserting variables inside **template literals (${} inside backticks)**.

Example:

```
let age = 25;
console.log(`I am ${age} years old.`);
```

Output:

```
"I am 25 years old."
```

10. How can you remove extra spaces from a string?

You can use trim(), trimStart(), and trimEnd().

Example:

```
let str = "   Hello, JavaScript!   ";
console.log(str.trim());       // Removes spaces from both sides
console.log(str.trimStart());  // Removes spaces from the start
console.log(str.trimEnd());    // Removes spaces from the end
```

Output:

```
"Hello, JavaScript!"
"Hello, JavaScript!   "
"   Hello, JavaScript!"
```

Summary of Key Concepts

- **Strings** store text and can be enclosed in "", '', or ````.
- **String methods** like slice(), split(), replace(), and trim() help in manipulating text.
- **Template literals** (${} inside backticks) allow string interpolation.
- **The spread (...) and rest (...) operators** help manipulate string-based arrays.
- **Regular expressions (RegEx)** are useful for pattern matching in strings.

1. Create a webpage where clicking a button changes the font size of a paragraph.
Solution:

```html
<!DOCTYPE html>
<html lang="en">
<head>
  <title>Change Font Size</title>
  <style>
    #text {
      font-size: 16px;
    }
  </style>
</head>
<body>
  <p id="text">This is a sample paragraph.</p>
  <button onclick="changeFontSize()">Increase Font Size</button>

  <script>
    function changeFontSize() {
      let para = document.getElementById("text");
      para.style.fontSize = "24px";
    }
  </script>
</body>
</html>
```

Explanation:
- The button uses onclick="changeFontSize()" to trigger the function.
- document.getElementById("text") selects the paragraph.
- style.fontSize = "24px" changes its font size.

2. Make a simple webpage where clicking a button adds a new list item in an existing list.
Solution:

```html
<!DOCTYPE html>
<html lang="en">
<head>
  <title>Add List Item</title>
```

```html
</head>
<body>
  <ul id="myList">
    <li>Item 1</li>
    <li>Item 2</li>
  </ul>
  <button onclick="addItem()">Add Item</button>

  <script>
    function addItem() {
      let list = document.getElementById("myList");
      let newItem = document.createElement("li");
      newItem.textContent = "New Item";
      list.appendChild(newItem);
    }
  </script>
</body>
</html>
```

Explanation:

- document.createElement("li") creates a new list item.
- textContent = "New Item" sets its text.
- appendChild(newItem) adds it to the list.

---

3. Create a page where clicking a button toggles the visibility of an image.

Solution:

```html
<!DOCTYPE html>
<html lang="en">
<head>
  <title>Toggle Image</title>
</head>
<body>
  <img id="myImage" src="https://via.placeholder.com/150"
alt="Sample Image">
  <button onclick="toggleImage()">Toggle Image</button>

  <script>
    function toggleImage() {
      let img = document.getElementById("myImage");
      if (img.style.display === "none") {
```

```
        img.style.display = "block";
      } else {
        img.style.display = "none";
      }
    }
  </script>
</body>
</html>
```

Explanation:

- style.display = "none" hides the image.
- Clicking the button toggles between "none" and "block".

<hr>

Short Answer Questions and Solutions

1. What is the DOM in JavaScript?
Answer:

The **Document Object Model (DOM)** is a tree-like structure representing a webpage. It allows JavaScript to interact with HTML elements dynamically.

<hr>

2. How does JavaScript interact with the DOM?
Answer:

JavaScript interacts with the DOM using methods like:
- document.getElementById("id") to access elements.
- document.createElement("tag") to create new elements.
- element.style.property = "value" to change styles.

Example:

```
document.getElementById("demo").style.color = "red";
```

<hr>

3. What does document.getElementById() do?
Answer:

It selects an element by its id.

Example:

```
let para = document.getElementById("text");
para.innerHTML = "Updated text!";
```

<hr>

4. How is querySelector different from getElementById?
Answer:

Method	Selects	Example
getElementById()	A single element by id	document.getElementById("myId")
querySelector()	The first element matching a CSS selector	document.querySelector(".myClass")

Example:

```
document.querySelector("p").style.color = "blue"; // Changes the first
<p> tag color
```

5. What property is used to change an element's text?
Answer:
innerHTML or textContent can be used.
Example:

```
document.getElementById("demo").innerHTML = "New text!";
```

6. How can you change the background color of an element?
Answer:
Using the style.backgroundColor property.
Example:

```
document.body.style.backgroundColor = "yellow";
```

7. How do you add a new element to the DOM using JavaScript?
Answer:
Use document.createElement() and appendChild().
Example:

```
let newPara = document.createElement("p");
newPara.textContent = "This is a new paragraph.";
document.body.appendChild(newPara);
```

8. What is innerHTML used for?
Answer:
innerHTML sets or gets the HTML content inside an element.
Example:

```
document.getElementById("content").innerHTML = "<b>Bold
Text</b>";
```

9. How do you remove an element from the DOM?
Answer:
Use removeChild() or remove().
Example:

```
let item = document.getElementById("myElement");
item.remove();  // Removes the element
```

10. What happens if an element with the given ID does not exist?
Answer:
document.getElementById("wrongId") returns null, and trying to manipulate it causes an error.
Example:

```
let missingElement = document.getElementById("nonExistent");
console.log(missingElement); // Output: null
```

Summary of Key Concepts

- **DOM** allows JavaScript to modify webpage content dynamically.
- getElementById() and querySelector() help select elements.
- innerHTML updates text, and style modifies CSS properties.
- createElement() and appendChild() add new elements.
- remove() deletes elements from the page.

Practical Exercises

1. Create a button that, when clicked, changes the background color of the entire page.

Solution:

```html
<!DOCTYPE html>
<html lang="en">
<head>
  <title>Change Background Color</title>
</head>
<body>
  <button id="colorButton">Change Background Color</button>

  <script>

document.getElementById("colorButton").addEventListener("click",
function() {
      document.body.style.backgroundColor = "lightblue";
    });
  </script>
</body>
</html>
```

Explanation:

- We use addEventListener("click", function() {...}) to listen for a button click.
- document.body.style.backgroundColor changes the page's background color.

2. Make a text box that displays a live word count as the user types.

Solution:

```html
<!DOCTYPE html>
<html lang="en">
<head>
  <title>Live Word Counter</title>
</head>
<body>
```

```html
    <textarea id="textBox" rows="5" cols="30" placeholder="Type
something..."></textarea>
  <p>Word Count: <span id="wordCount">0</span></p>

  <script>
    document.getElementById("textBox").addEventListener("input",
function() {
      let text = this.value.trim();
      let words = text.length > 0 ? text.split(/\s+/).length : 0;
      document.getElementById("wordCount").innerText = words;
    });
  </script>
</body>
</html>
```

Explanation:
- The input event triggers whenever the user types.
- .split(/\s+/) splits words based on spaces.
- trim() removes extra spaces to avoid incorrect counting.

---

3. Build a simple To-Do List where clicking on a task removes it from the list.
Solution:

```html
<!DOCTYPE html>
<html lang="en">
<head>
  <title>To-Do List</title>
</head>
<body>
  <input type="text" id="taskInput" placeholder="Add a task">
  <button id="addTask">Add Task</button>
  <ul id="taskList"></ul>

  <script>
    document.getElementById("addTask").addEventListener("click",
function() {
      let taskInput = document.getElementById("taskInput");
      let taskText = taskInput.value.trim();

      if (taskText !== "") {
        let li = document.createElement("li");
```

```
      li.textContent = taskText;
      li.addEventListener("click", function() {
        this.remove();  // Removes task when clicked
      });

      document.getElementById("taskList").appendChild(li);
      taskInput.value = ""; // Clear input field
    }
  });
</script>
</body>
</html>
```

Explanation:
- A new <li> element is created when clicking "Add Task".
- Clicking the task removes it using .remove().

Short Answer Questions and Solutions

1. What is an event in JavaScript?

An **event** is an action that occurs on a webpage, such as a user **clicking a button, typing text, or scrolling**. JavaScript can listen for these events and respond accordingly.

Example:

```
document.getElementById("btn").addEventListener("click", function()
{
    alert("Button clicked!");
});
```

---

2. How do you attach an event listener to a button?

You can attach an event listener using addEventListener().

Example:

```
document.getElementById("myButton").addEventListener("click",
function() {
    console.log("Button Clicked!");
});
"click" is the event name.
```

- The function inside addEventListener() runs when the button is clicked.

3. What is the purpose of addEventListener()?

- addEventListener() **binds an event** (e.g., "click", "keyup", "mouseover") to an element.
- It allows multiple event listeners on the same element without overwriting them.

Example:

```
document.getElementById("box").addEventListener("mouseover",
function() {
   console.log("Mouse Over Detected!");
});
```

4. Explain what happens in a mouseover event.

The mouseover event triggers when the **mouse pointer enters an element**.

Example:

```
document.getElementById("hoverDiv").addEventListener("mouseover
", function() {
   this.style.backgroundColor = "yellow";
});
```

Explanation: The background turns yellow when the user hovers over hoverDiv.

5. How does JavaScript detect keypress events?

JavaScript detects keypress events using keydown, keyup, or keypress events.

Example:

```
document.addEventListener("keydown", function(event) {
   console.log("Key pressed:", event.key);
});
```

Explanation:

- event.key returns the key the user pressed.

6. What is the event object?

The **event object (event or e)** contains information about the event that occurred, like:

- event.type → Type of event (e.g., "click", "keydown").
- event.target → The element that triggered the event.

Example:

```
document.addEventListener("click", function(event) {
  console.log("Clicked element:", event.target);
});
```

---

7. Why do we use event delegation?

Event delegation allows handling multiple child elements using a **single parent event listener** instead of adding an event to each child individually.
Example:

```
document.getElementById("parentList").addEventListener("click",
function(event) {
  if (event.target.tagName === "LI") {
    event.target.style.color = "red";
  }
});
```

Advantages:
- **Improves performance** for large lists.
- **Handles dynamically added elements**.

---

8. What property gives the element that triggered an event?

The event.target property returns the element that triggered the event.
Example:

```
document.getElementById("myDiv").addEventListener("click",
function(event) {
  console.log("Clicked Element:", event.target.tagName);
});
```

---

9. How can JavaScript prevent a form from submitting if an input is incorrect?

We use event.preventDefault() inside the form's submit event.
Example:

```
document.getElementById("myForm").addEventListener("submit",
function(event) {
  let inputValue = document.getElementById("nameInput").value;
  if (inputValue === "") {
    alert("Name cannot be empty!");
    event.preventDefault(); // Prevent form submission
  }
});
```

10. Write the JavaScript code to detect when a user right-clicks on a webpage.

Right-clicks trigger the "contextmenu" event.

Example:

```javascript
document.addEventListener("contextmenu", function(event) {
    event.preventDefault(); // Prevent default right-click menu
    alert("Right-click detected!");
});
```

Summary of Key Concepts

- **Events** are user interactions like clicks and keypresses.
- **addEventListener()** binds events to elements.
- **The event object** provides details about an event.
- **Event delegation** improves efficiency when handling many elements.
- **preventDefault()** stops default behaviors (like form submission or right-click menu).

Assignment Solutions
Exercise 1: Countdown Timer
Create a countdown timer that starts from 10 and decreases every second
until it reaches 0.
Solution:

```
let count = 10;

let countdown = setInterval(() => {
  console.log(count);
  count--;

  if (count < 0) {
    clearInterval(countdown);
    console.log("Time's up!");
  }
}, 1000);
```

Output:

```
10
9
8
7
6
5
4
3
2
1
0
Time's up!
```

Explanation:
- We use setInterval() to decrease the countdown every second
  (1000ms).
- Once count becomes -1, clearInterval() stops the timer.

Exercise 2: Blinking Text

Make a text blink every 500ms using setInterval().

Solution:

```html
<!DOCTYPE html>
<html lang="en">
<head>
  <title>Blinking Text</title>
</head>
<body>
  <h1 id="blinkText">Hello, World!</h1>

  <script>
    let text = document.getElementById("blinkText");
    let isVisible = true;

    setInterval(() => {
      text.style.visibility = isVisible ? "hidden" : "visible";
      isVisible = !isVisible;
    }, 500);
  </script>
</body>
</html>
```

Explanation:
- We use setInterval() to change the text visibility every 500ms.
- visibility: hidden makes the text disappear, and visibility: visible makes it reappear.

Exercise 3: Stop a Timer

Create a button that starts a timer and another button that stops it.

Solution:

```html
<!DOCTYPE html>
<html lang="en">
<head>
  <title>Start & Stop Timer</title>
</head>
<body>
  <button id="start">Start Timer</button>
  <button id="stop">Stop Timer</button>
  <p id="timer">0</p>
```

```
    <script>
      let counter = 0;
      let timer;

      document.getElementById("start").addEventListener("click", () =>
{
          timer = setInterval(() => {
              document.getElementById("timer").textContent = counter++;
          }, 1000);
      });

      document.getElementById("stop").addEventListener("click", () =>
{
          clearInterval(timer);
      });
    </script>
</body>
</html>
```

Explanation:

- Clicking **Start Timer** begins a counter using setInterval().
- Clicking **Stop Timer** stops the counter using clearInterval().

Short Answer Questions and Explanations

1. What is setTimeout() used for?

setTimeout() executes a function **after a specified delay** (in milliseconds).
Example:

```
setTimeout(() => console.log("Hello after 2 seconds"), 2000);
```

Output:

```
Hello after 2 seconds (appears after 2 seconds)
```

---

2. How does setInterval() work?

setInterval() repeatedly calls a function **at fixed time intervals**.
Example:

```
setInterval(() => console.log("Repeating every second"), 1000);
```

Output:

Repeating every second

(Repeated infinitely every second)

---

3. What is the difference between setTimeout() and setInterval()?

Feature	setTimeout()	setInterval()
Execution	Runs once after a delay	Repeats at fixed intervals
Stops when?	After execution	When clearInterval() is used
Example	setTimeout(myFunction, 2000);	setInterval(myFunction, 2000);

---

4. How can you stop a running setTimeout()?
Use clearTimeout() and pass the timeout ID.
Example:

```
let timer = setTimeout(() => console.log("This will not run"), 3000);
clearTimeout(timer);
```

Explanation:
- clearTimeout(timer) cancels the timeout before it executes.

---

5. How can you stop an ongoing setInterval()?
Use clearInterval().
Example:

```
let interval = setInterval(() => console.log("Repeating..."), 1000);
clearInterval(interval);
```

Explanation:
- clearInterval(interval) stops the repeating function.

---

6. What unit is used for specifying delay in setTimeout()?
The delay is specified in **milliseconds (ms)**.
- 1000 ms = 1 second

Example:

```
setTimeout(() => console.log("Runs after 1 second"), 1000);
```

---

7. Write an example of setTimeout() that changes text after 2 seconds.
Solution:

```html
<p id="text">Original Text</p>

<script>
setTimeout(() => {
  document.getElementById("text").textContent = "Text changed!";
}, 2000);
</script>
```

Explanation:
- The text changes after **2 seconds**.

---

8. What is the use of clearInterval()?
It **stops** a repeating setInterval() function.
Example:

```javascript
let counter = setInterval(() => console.log("Repeating..."), 1000);
clearInterval(counter);
```

Explanation:
- clearInterval(counter) stops the interval.

---

9. How can JavaScript timing functions be used for animations?
- setInterval() or setTimeout() can create animations by updating CSS styles at intervals.

Example: Moving a box:

```html
<div id="box" style="width:50px; height:50px; background:red;
position:absolute;"></div>

<script>
let pos = 0;
let move = setInterval(() => {
  pos += 5;
  document.getElementById("box").style.left = pos + "px";

  if (pos >= 200) clearInterval(move);
}, 100);
</script>
```

Explanation:
- Moves the box **5 pixels every 100ms** until it reaches 200px.

---

10. Give one practical use case for setInterval().

Example: Live Clock

```html
<p id="clock"></p>

<script>
setInterval(() => {
  document.getElementById("clock").textContent = new
Date().toLocaleTimeString();
}, 1000);
</script>
```

Explanation:
- Updates the clock **every second**.

Summary of Key Concepts

- setTimeout() **runs once after a delay**.
- setInterval() **runs repeatedly at intervals**.
- clearTimeout() **cancels a timeout before execution**.
- clearInterval() **stops a repeating interval**.
- JavaScript timers are used for **animations, clocks, countdowns, and UI updates**.

Assignment Solutions

1. Write a function that takes two numbers and divides them. If the second number is 0, throw an error saying "Division by zero is not allowed".

```javascript
function divideNumbers(a, b) {
   if (b === 0) {
      throw new Error("Division by zero is not allowed");
   }
   return a / b;
}


// Testing the function
try {
   console.log(divideNumbers(10, 2)); // Output: 5
   console.log(divideNumbers(8, 0));  // This will throw an error
} catch (error) {
   console.error(error.message);
}
```

Explanation:
- The function divideNumbers(a, b) checks if b is 0.
- If b === 0, it throws an error using throw new Error().
- The try...catch block **catches** the error and prints an error message.

2. Create a simple calculator program using try...catch. It should accept two numbers and an operation (+, -, , /). Handle cases where the user enters an invalid number or an invalid operation.

```javascript
function calculator(num1, num2, operation) {
   try {
     if (isNaN(num1) || isNaN(num2)) {
        throw new Error("Invalid number input");
     }

     switch (operation) {
        case "+":
```

```javascript
      return num1 + num2;
    case "-":
      return num1 - num2;
    case "*":
      return num1 * num2;
    case "/":
      if (num2 === 0) {
        throw new Error("Division by zero is not allowed");
      }
      return num1 / num2;
    default:
      throw new Error("Invalid operation");
    }
  } catch (error) {
    return `Error: ${error.message}`;
  }
}

// Testing the function
console.log(calculator(10, 5, "+"));  // Output: 15
console.log(calculator(10, 0, "/"));  // Output: Error: Division by zero is not allowed
console.log(calculator(10, "a", "*")); // Output: Error: Invalid number input
console.log(calculator(10, 5, "^"));  // Output: Error: Invalid operation
```

Explanation:
- The function calculator() uses try...catch to handle errors.
- It throws an error if inputs are **not numbers**, if **division by zero** occurs, or if the **operation is invalid**.

---

3. Use debugger; in a function that calculates the sum of an array of numbers. Run it in the browser's DevTools to inspect variables.

```javascript
function sumArray(numbers) {
  debugger; // Pause execution for debugging
  return numbers.reduce((sum, num) => sum + num, 0);
}

// Testing in the browser's DevTools
console.log(sumArray([1, 2, 3, 4, 5])); // Output: 15
```

Explanation:
- The debugger; statement **pauses execution** at that point.
- Open **Developer Tools (F12 in Chrome)** and go to the **Console tab**.
- Run the function and inspect variables step by step.

Short Answer Questions and Explanations

1. What is error handling in JavaScript?

Error handling in JavaScript refers to methods used to **catch, handle, and prevent errors** in code execution. It ensures programs run smoothly without crashing unexpectedly.

Example using try...catch:

```javascript
try {
    let x = undefinedVariable; // Causes an error
} catch (error) {
    console.log("An error occurred:", error.message);
}
```

2. Name three types of JavaScript errors.
1. **Syntax Errors:** Occur due to incorrect JavaScript syntax.
2. console.log("Hello" // Missing closing parenthesis
3. **Reference Errors:** Occur when accessing an undefined variable.
4. console.log(myVar); // myVar is not defined
5. **Type Errors:** Occur when performing an operation on an incompatible type.
6. let num = 10;
7. num.toUpperCase(); // TypeError: num.toUpperCase is not a function

3. What does the try block do?

The try block contains the code that might cause an error. If an error occurs, JavaScript stops executing the try block and jumps to the catch block.

Example:

```javascript
try {
    let x = y; // y is not defined
} catch (error) {
    console.log("Error caught:", error.message);
}
```

4. How does the catch block work?

The catch block **captures and handles errors** that occur inside the try block.

Example:

```
try {
    let result = 5 / 0;
} catch (error) {
    console.log("Something went wrong:", error.message);
}
```

5. What is the purpose of the finally block?

The finally block **executes regardless of whether an error occurs or not**.

Example:

```
try {
    console.log("Trying...");
    throw new Error("Oops!");
} catch (error) {
    console.log("Error caught:", error.message);
} finally {
    console.log("Finally block runs no matter what!");
}
```

Output:

```
Trying...
Error caught: Oops!
Finally block runs no matter what!
```

6. What happens if an error is not caught using try...catch?

If an error is not caught, JavaScript stops execution, and an **uncaught error message** appears in the console.

Example:

```
console.log(5 / undefinedVar); // ReferenceError: undefinedVar is not defined
```

7. How do you manually throw an error in JavaScript?

Use throw new Error("Message") to manually create an error.

Example:

```
function checkAge(age) {
  if (age < 18) {
    throw new Error("You must be 18 or older");
  }
  return "Access granted";
}

try {
  console.log(checkAge(16)); // Error: You must be 18 or older
} catch (error) {
  console.log(error.message);
}
```

8. What is the purpose of console.log() in debugging?

console.log() prints values to the console for debugging.

Example:

```
let name = "Alice";
console.log("User name is:", name);
```

9. How can you pause JavaScript execution using the browser's debugger?

You can **pause execution** by:

1. Using debugger; in code.
2. Adding breakpoints in **Developer Tools → Sources Tab**.

```
Example:
function testDebug() {
  let a = 10;
  debugger;  // Execution pauses here
  let b = 20;
  return a + b;
}
testDebug();
```

10. Give an example of an error message when trying to use an undefined variable.

Example:

```
console.log(nonExistentVar);
```

Error Message:
ReferenceError: nonExistentVar is not defined

Summary of Key Concepts

- try...catch helps prevent JavaScript from crashing on errors.
- throw manually raises errors.
- finally runs **always**, regardless of errors.
- console.log() helps debug by printing values.
- debugger; pauses execution for **step-by-step** debugging.

Assignment Solutions

1. Convert the following function into an arrow function:

Given Function:

```
function multiply(a, b) {
    return a * b;
}
```

Solution (Arrow Function):

```
const multiply = (a, b) => a * b;
console.log(multiply(5, 3));
```

Output:

```
15
```

Explanation:

- Arrow functions use => instead of the function keyword.
- The {} and return keyword can be omitted if there's only one expression.

2. Use the spread operator to merge these two objects:

Given Objects:

```
let obj1 = { a: 1, b: 2 };
let obj2 = { c: 3, d: 4 };
```

Solution (Using Spread Operator):

```
let mergedObj = { ...obj1, ...obj2 };
console.log(mergedObj);
```

Output:

```
{ a: 1, b: 2, c: 3, d: 4 }
```

Explanation:

- The spread operator (...) expands objects and allows easy merging.
- The new object contains all properties from obj1 and obj2.

3. Use destructuring to extract values from this array:
Given Array:

```
let fruits = ["Apple", "Banana", "Mango"];
```

Solution (Destructuring):

```
let [fruit1, fruit2, fruit3] = fruits;
console.log(fruit1, fruit2, fruit3);
```

Output:

```
Apple Banana Mango
```

Explanation:
- Destructuring allows assigning array values directly to variables.
- fruit1 = "Apple", fruit2 = "Banana", fruit3 = "Mango".

Short Answer Questions & Solutions

1. What is the difference between var, let, and const?

Keyword	Scope	Reassignment	Redeclaration	Hoisting
var	Function-scoped	Yes	Yes	Hoisted with undefined
let	Block-scoped	Yes	No	Hoisted but not initialized
const	Block-scoped	No	No	Hoisted but not initialized

---

2. Why is let preferred over var?
- let is **block-scoped**, preventing unintended variable access.
- var is **function-scoped**, which may cause issues in loops.
- let does **not allow redeclaration**, reducing errors.

Example:

```
for (var i = 0; i < 3; i++) {
    setTimeout(() => console.log(i), 1000);
}
// Output: 3 3 3 (because var is function-scoped)
```

Using let:

```
for (let i = 0; i < 3; i++) {
```

```
    setTimeout(() => console.log(i), 1000);
}
// Output: 0 1 2 (because let is block-scoped)
```

---

3. What is the main advantage of arrow functions?

- **Shorter syntax** than regular functions.
- **Do not have their own this**, making them useful inside callbacks.

Example:

```
const person = {
  name: "John",
  greet: function() {
    setTimeout(() => {
      console.log("Hello, " + this.name);
    }, 1000);
  }
};
person.greet();
```

Output:

```
Hello, John
```

Explanation:

- The arrow function inherits this from greet().
- If a normal function was used inside setTimeout(), this would be undefined.

---

4. How do you use the spread operator with arrays?

The spread operator (...) expands array elements.

Example:

```
let arr1 = [1, 2, 3];
let arr2 = [4, 5, 6];
let mergedArray = [...arr1, ...arr2];
console.log(mergedArray);
```

Output:

```
[1, 2, 3, 4, 5, 6]
```

---

5. What does the rest operator do?

The rest operator (...) collects multiple values into an array.

Example:

```
function sum(...numbers) {
  return numbers.reduce((total, num) => total + num, 0);
}
console.log(sum(2, 3, 4));
```

Output:

```
9
```

Explanation:

- The function accepts multiple arguments as an array (numbers).

---

6. How does destructuring simplify code?

Destructuring allows extracting values easily from arrays and objects.

Example:

```
let person = { name: "Alice", age: 25 };
let { name, age } = person;
console.log(name, age);
```

Output:

```
Alice 25
```

Without destructuring:

```
let name = person.name;
let age = person.age;
```

---

7. Can you reassign a variable declared with const?

No, a const variable **cannot be reassigned**.

Example:

```
const x = 10;
x = 20; // Error: Assignment to constant variable
```

---

8. What happens if you redeclare a let variable?

Redeclaring a let variable in the same scope throws an error.

Example:

```
let a = 5;
let a = 10; // Error: Identifier 'a' has already been declared
```

9. How do you copy an object using the spread operator?
The spread operator (...) can be used to create a shallow copy.
Example:

```
let obj1 = { name: "Alice", age: 25 };
let obj2 = { ...obj1 };
console.log(obj2);
```

Output:

```
{ name: "Alice", age: 25 }
```

10. What will be the output of the following code?

```
const [x, y] = [10, 20];
console.log(x, y);
```

Output:

```
10 20
```

Explanation:
- The array [10, 20] is **destructured** into x = 10 and y = 20.

Summary of Key Concepts

- **Arrow Functions (=>)** → Shorter, no this.
- **Spread Operator (...)** → Expands arrays/objects.
- **Rest Operator (...)** → Collects multiple function arguments into an array.
- **Destructuring** → Simplifies extracting values from arrays/objects.
- **var vs. let vs. const** → let is block-scoped, var is function-scoped.
- **Objects and Arrays can be copied using the spread operator (...).**

Assignment Solutions (Practical Exercises)
1. Write a function using a callback to print "Hello" after 3 seconds.
Solution:

```javascript
function delayedHello(callback) {
  setTimeout(() => {
    callback("Hello");
  }, 3000);
}

function printMessage(message) {
  console.log(message);
}

// Call the function with a callback
delayedHello(printMessage);
```

Output after 3 seconds:

```
Hello
```

Explanation:
   - setTimeout() delays execution by 3 seconds.
   - A callback function (printMessage) is passed to delayedHello(), which calls it after 3 seconds.

2. Create a Promise that resolves with "Success!" after 1 second and use .then() to print the message.
Solution:

```javascript
let myPromise = new Promise((resolve) => {
  setTimeout(() => {
    resolve("Success!");
  }, 1000);
});

myPromise.then((message) => console.log(message));
```

Output after 1 second:

```
Success!
```

Explanation:
- A Promise is created that resolves after 1 second.
- .then() executes once the promise is resolved, printing "Success!".

---

3. Write an async/await function to wait 2 seconds before printing "Async function executed!".

Solution:

```
async function delayedExecution() {
    await new Promise(resolve => setTimeout(resolve, 2000));
    console.log("Async function executed!");
}

delayedExecution();
```

Output after 2 seconds:

```
Async function executed!
```

Explanation:
- await pauses the function execution until the Promise (setTimeout) is resolved.
- The message is printed after 2 seconds.

Short Questions and Solutions

1. What is synchronous and asynchronous execution?

Answer:
- **Synchronous execution** runs **line by line**, blocking further code until the current line is finished.
- **Asynchronous execution** allows the program to **continue running** while waiting for a process (like fetching data).

Example:

```
console.log("Start");
setTimeout(() => console.log("Async Task"), 1000);
console.log("End");
```

Output:

```
Start
```

```
End
Async Task (after 1 second)
```

---

2. What is the purpose of setTimeout()?

Answer:

setTimeout() is used to **execute a function after a specified delay**.

Example:

```
setTimeout(() => console.log("Hello after 2 seconds"), 2000);
```

Output after 2 seconds:

```
Hello after 2 seconds
```

---

3. What is a callback function?

Answer:

A **callback function** is a function passed as an argument to another function to be **executed later**.

Example:

```
function greet(name, callback) {
  console.log("Hello, " + name);
  callback();
}

function sayGoodbye() {
  console.log("Goodbye!");
}

greet("Alice", sayGoodbye);
```

Output:

```
Hello, Alice
Goodbye!
```

---

4. What is "callback hell"?

Answer:

"Callback hell" happens when multiple **nested callbacks** make code **hard to read and maintain**.

Example of Callback Hell:

```javascript
setTimeout(() => {
  console.log("Step 1");
  setTimeout(() => {
    console.log("Step 2");
    setTimeout(() => {
      console.log("Step 3");
    }, 1000);
  }, 1000);
}, 1000);
```

Solution: Use **Promises** or **async/await**.

---

5. What are the three states of a Promise?

Answer:

A JavaScript Promise has three states:

1. **Pending** – Initial state, waiting for resolution or rejection.
2. **Fulfilled** – Promise resolved successfully.
3. **Rejected** – Promise failed.

Example:

```javascript
let promise = new Promise((resolve, reject) => {
  setTimeout(() => resolve("Done!"), 1000);
});

promise.then(console.log);
```

---

6. How do we handle errors in Promises?

Answer:

Use **.catch()** to handle errors in Promises.

Example:

```javascript
let promise = new Promise((resolve, reject) => {
  reject("Error occurred!");
});

promise
  .then(console.log)
  .catch(error => console.log("Caught:", error));
```

Output:

```
Caught: Error occurred!
```

7. What does async do?

Answer:

- The async keyword makes a function return a **Promise**.
- It enables **await** inside the function.

Example:

```
async function example() {
   return "Hello, Async!";
}


example().then(console.log);
```

Output:

```
Hello, Async!
```

---

8. Why is await useful?

Answer:

- await makes JavaScript **wait** until a Promise resolves.
- It **removes the need for .then()**.

Example:

```
async function getData() {
   let data = await
fetch("https://jsonplaceholder.typicode.com/todos/1");
   let result = await data.json();
   console.log(result);
}
getData();
```

---

9. What is the difference between .then() and await?

Feature	.then()	await
Type	Used with Promises	Used inside async functions
Syntax	.then(result => console.log(result))	let result = await promise
Readability	Can cause nested .then() chains	More readable like synchronous code

Example with .then()

```
fetch("https://jsonplaceholder.typicode.com/todos/1")
   .then(response => response.json())
```

```
  .then(data => console.log(data));
```

Example with await

```
async function fetchData() {
  let response = await
fetch("https://jsonplaceholder.typicode.com/todos/1");
  let data = await response.json();
  console.log(data);
}
fetchData();
```

10. Why is async/await preferred over callbacks?
Answer:

- **Improves readability** (no callback nesting).
- **Easier error handling** with try...catch.
- **Looks like synchronous code** but is still asynchronous.

Example:

❌ **With Callbacks (Hard to Read)**

```
function getData(callback) {
  setTimeout(() => callback("Data received"), 1000);
}
getData(result => console.log(result));
```

✅ **With Async/Await (Cleaner)**

```
async function getData() {
  let result = await new Promise(resolve => setTimeout(() =>
resolve("Data received"), 1000));
  console.log(result);
}
getData();
```

Summary of Key Concepts

- **Callbacks** execute functions after a task is completed.
- **Promises** handle asynchronous tasks and have .then() and .catch().
- **async/await** makes asynchronous code easier to read.
- **Avoid "callback hell"** by using Promises or async/await.
- **await pauses execution** until a Promise resolves.

Assignment Solutions

Exercise 1: Fetch Random Dog Images

Problem Statement:
Write a JavaScript program to fetch a random dog image from the API:
 URL: https://dog.ceo/api/breeds/image/random
Display it inside an <img> tag in HTML.

Solution:

```html
<!DOCTYPE html>
<html lang="en">
<head>
  <meta charset="UTF-8">
  <meta name="viewport" content="width=device-width, initial-scale=1.0">
  <title>Random Dog Image</title>
</head>
<body>
  <h2>Random Dog Image</h2>
  <button onclick="fetchDogImage()">Get Random Dog</button>
  <br><br>
  <img id="dogImage" src="" alt="Random Dog" width="300">

  <script>
    function fetchDogImage() {
      fetch("https://dog.ceo/api/breeds/image/random")
        .then(response => response.json()) // Convert response to JSON
        .then(data => {
          document.getElementById("dogImage").src = data.message;
        })
        .catch(error => console.error("Error fetching dog image:", error));
    }
  </script>
</body>
```

```
</html>
```

Expected Output:

- Clicking the button **fetches a random dog image** and displays it inside the <img> tag.

Exercise 2: Fetch and Display Jokes

Problem Statement:
Fetch a random joke from https://official-joke-api.appspot.com/random_joke
Display the joke on a webpage.

Solution:

```html
<!DOCTYPE html>
<html lang="en">
<head>
  <meta charset="UTF-8">
  <meta name="viewport" content="width=device-width, initial-scale=1.0">
  <title>Random Joke Generator</title>
</head>
<body>
  <h2>Random Joke</h2>
  <button onclick="fetchJoke()">Get a Joke</button>
  <p id="joke"></p>

  <script>
    function fetchJoke() {
      fetch("https://official-joke-api.appspot.com/random_joke")
        .then(response => response.json())
        .then(data => {
            document.getElementById("joke").innerHTML = data.setup
+ "<br>" + data.punchline;
        })
        .catch(error => console.error("Error fetching joke:", error));
    }
  </script>
</body>
</html>
```

Expected Output:

- Clicking the button **fetches a joke** and displays it inside the <p>
  tag.

Exercise 3: Fetch and Search User Data

Problem Statement:
Modify the random user API example to allow users to search for a user by
country.
URL: https://randomuser.me/api/

Solution:

```
<!DOCTYPE html>
<html lang="en">
<head>
  <meta charset="UTF-8">
  <meta name="viewport" content="width=device-width, initial-
scale=1.0">
  <title>Search User by Country</title>
</head>
<body>
  <h2>Search Random User by Country</h2>
  <input type="text" id="countryInput" placeholder="Enter country
name">
  <button onclick="fetchUser()">Find User</button>
  <p id="userInfo"></p>

  <script>
    function fetchUser() {
      fetch("https://randomuser.me/api/")
        .then(response => response.json())
        .then(data => {
          let user = data.results[0];
          let enteredCountry =
document.getElementById("countryInput").value.toLowerCase();
          let userCountry = user.location.country.toLowerCase();

          if (enteredCountry === userCountry) {
```

```
                document.getElementById("userInfo").innerHTML =
`Name: ${user.name.first} ${user.name.last}<br>Country:
${user.location.country}`;
            } else {
                document.getElementById("userInfo").innerHTML = "No
user found from that country!";
            }
        })
        .catch(error => console.error("Error fetching user:", error));
    }
  </script>
</body>
</html>
```

Expected Output:

- Enter a country name, click the button, and a **random user** from that country (if found) is displayed.

Short Answer Questions and Explanations

1. What is the Fetch API?

The Fetch API is a **modern way** to make HTTP requests (GET, POST, etc.) in JavaScript. It allows web applications to fetch and send data from APIs asynchronously.

Example:

```
fetch("https://api.example.com/data")
   .then(response => response.json())
   .then(data => console.log(data));
```

---

2. What does .then() do in the Fetch API?

- .then() is used to **handle the response** from a fetch request.

- It processes the response **asynchronously**.

Example:

```
fetch("https://api.example.com")
```

```
    .then(response => response.json()) // Convert response to JSON
    .then(data => console.log(data));  // Handle the data
```

3. How do you handle errors in Fetch?

Use .catch() to handle errors.

Example:

```
fetch("https://api.example.com")
    .then(response => response.json())
    .then(data => console.log(data))
    .catch(error => console.error("Error fetching data:", error));
```

4. What is JSON?

JSON (JavaScript Object Notation) is a lightweight data format **used to store and transfer data** between servers and clients.

Example JSON:

```
{
   "name": "John",
   "age": 25
}
```

5. How do you convert JSON data into a JavaScript object?

Use JSON.parse() or .json() in Fetch.

Example:

```
let jsonString = '{"name": "John", "age": 25}';
let user = JSON.parse(jsonString);
console.log(user.name); // Output: John
```

6. What does fetch("URL") return?

It returns a **Promise** that resolves to a Response object.

Example:

```
fetch("https://api.example.com")
  .then(response => console.log(response));
```

7. What are some real-life use cases of Fetch API?

- Fetching **weather data** from APIs.

- Fetching **stock market prices**.

- Displaying **news articles** from APIs.

- Uploading **user data** to a server.

8. How do you display fetched data on a webpage?

You can use document.getElementById().innerHTML.

Example:

```
fetch("https://api.example.com/data")
  .then(response => response.json())
  .then(data => {
    document.getElementById("output").innerHTML = data.message;
  });
```

9. What is an API?

An API (Application Programming Interface) is a **set of rules** that allows software to communicate.

Example:

- https://dog.ceo/api/breeds/image/random API returns a **random dog image**.

10. How do you check if an API response is successful?

Check response.ok or response.status.

Example:

```javascript
fetch("https://api.example.com")
  .then(response => {
    if (!response.ok) {
      throw new Error("Network error!");
    }
    return response.json();
  })
  .then(data => console.log(data))
  .catch(error => console.error(error));
```

Practical Exercises Solutions

1. Create a Simple To-Do List App Using LocalStorage

A **to-do list** where tasks persist even after refreshing the page.

```html
<!DOCTYPE html>
<html lang="en">
<head>
  <title>To-Do List</title>
</head>
<body>
  <h2>To-Do List</h2>
  <input type="text" id="taskInput" placeholder="Enter a task">
  <button onclick="addTask()">Add Task</button>
  <ul id="taskList"></ul>

  <script>
    // Load tasks from LocalStorage
    function loadTasks() {
      let tasks = JSON.parse(localStorage.getItem("tasks")) || [];
      let taskList = document.getElementById("taskList");
      taskList.innerHTML = "";
      tasks.forEach((task, index) => {
        let li = document.createElement("li");
        li.textContent = task;
        let btn = document.createElement("button");
        btn.textContent = "✖";
        btn.onclick = () => removeTask(index);
        li.appendChild(btn);
        taskList.appendChild(li);
      });
    }

    // Add task to list and save in LocalStorage
    function addTask() {
      let taskInput = document.getElementById("taskInput").value;
      if (taskInput === "") return;
      let tasks = JSON.parse(localStorage.getItem("tasks")) || [];
```

```html
      tasks.push(taskInput);
      localStorage.setItem("tasks", JSON.stringify(tasks));
      document.getElementById("taskInput").value = "";
      loadTasks();
    }

    // Remove task from LocalStorage
    function removeTask(index) {
      let tasks = JSON.parse(localStorage.getItem("tasks"));
      tasks.splice(index, 1);
      localStorage.setItem("tasks", JSON.stringify(tasks));
      loadTasks();
    }

    loadTasks(); // Load tasks when the page loads
  </script>
</body>
</html>
```

Explanation:

- Tasks are stored in **LocalStorage** using localStorage.setItem().
- The page **loads tasks** from LocalStorage when it loads.
- Clicking "Add Task" updates the list and saves the task.
- Clicking " ✕ " removes a task from **LocalStorage**.

---

2. Create a Theme Switcher (Light/Dark Mode) with LocalStorage

A **light/dark theme switcher** that remembers user preferences.

```html
<!DOCTYPE html>
<html lang="en">
<head>
  <title>Theme Switcher</title>
  <style>
    body.dark-mode { background-color: black; color: white; }
  </style>
</head>
<body>
  <button onclick="toggleTheme()">Toggle Light/Dark
Mode</button>

  <script>
    function loadTheme() {
```

```
    let theme = localStorage.getItem("theme");
    if (theme === "dark") {
      document.body.classList.add("dark-mode");
    }
  }

  function toggleTheme() {
    document.body.classList.toggle("dark-mode");
    let theme = document.body.classList.contains("dark-mode") ?
"dark" : "light";
    localStorage.setItem("theme", theme);
  }

  loadTheme(); // Load theme on page load
</script>
</body>
</html>
```

Explanation:
- Theme is stored in **LocalStorage** as "dark" or "light".
- When the page loads, the stored theme is applied.
- Clicking the button toggles the theme and updates **LocalStorage**.

---

3. Develop a Form Autosave Feature Using LocalStorage
A **form that saves input text** even after refreshing the page.

```
<!DOCTYPE html>
<html lang="en">
<head>
  <title>Form Autosave</title>
</head>
<body>
  <h2>Autosave Form</h2>
  <textarea id="textInput" placeholder="Type
something..."></textarea>

  <script>
    let textInput = document.getElementById("textInput");

    // Load saved text
    textInput.value = localStorage.getItem("savedText") || "";
```

```
    // Save text when user types
    textInput.addEventListener("input", () => {
      localStorage.setItem("savedText", textInput.value);
    });
  </script>
</body>
</html>
```

Explanation:

- The text in the <textarea> is **saved in LocalStorage** on every input change.
- When the page reloads, the saved text is restored.

---

1. What is LocalStorage in JavaScript?

LocalStorage is a web storage feature that allows storing **key-value pairs** in a web browser with **no expiration time**. The data remains even after **closing the browser**.

Example:

```
localStorage.setItem("username", "JohnDoe");
console.log(localStorage.getItem("username")); // "JohnDoe"
```

---

2. How does SessionStorage differ from LocalStorage?

Feature	LocalStorage	SessionStorage
Data Expiration	Never expires	Removed when the browser is closed
Storage Limit	5MB	5MB
Accessibility	Available across all tabs/windows	Limited to the tab where it was created

Example:

```
sessionStorage.setItem("tempData", "Session Data");
console.log(sessionStorage.getItem("tempData")); // "Session Data"
```

---

3. How can you store and retrieve data from LocalStorage?

Storing Data:

```
localStorage.setItem("user", "Alice");
```

Retrieving Data:

```
let user = localStorage.getItem("user");
console.log(user); // "Alice"
```

---

4. How do you delete a single item from LocalStorage?

Use removeItem():

```
localStorage.removeItem("user");
```

---

5. What happens to data in SessionStorage when the browser is closed?

Data stored in **SessionStorage is deleted** when the browser or tab is closed.

---

6. Why do we use JSON.stringify() and JSON.parse() with LocalStorage?

LocalStorage **only stores strings**. To store objects/arrays, we convert them to a string using JSON.stringify() and retrieve them using JSON.parse().
Example:

```
let user = { name: "Alice", age: 25 };
localStorage.setItem("user", JSON.stringify(user));

let retrievedUser = JSON.parse(localStorage.getItem("user"));
console.log(retrievedUser.name); // "Alice"
```

---

7. How can LocalStorage help in creating a theme switcher?

By saving the **theme choice** (light/dark) in LocalStorage and applying it when the page loads.
Example:

```
localStorage.setItem("theme", "dark");
```

---

8. What is the storage limit of LocalStorage?

Most browsers allow **5MB** of storage per origin (domain).

---

9. Can LocalStorage store JavaScript objects directly? Why or why not?

No, LocalStorage **can only store strings**. Objects must be converted using JSON.stringify().

---

10. Write JavaScript code to store and retrieve a user's age from LocalStorage.

```javascript
// Store age
localStorage.setItem("age", "30");

// Retrieve age
let age = localStorage.getItem("age");
console.log(age); // Output: "30"
```

Summary of Key Concepts

- **LocalStorage vs. SessionStorage**: LocalStorage persists; SessionStorage is tab-specific.
- **Use JSON.stringify() to store objects** in LocalStorage.
- **Data in LocalStorage does not expire unless manually removed.**
- **Useful for saving themes, forms, and user preferences.**

Assignment Solutions
1. Create a Student Class
Solution:

```javascript
class Student {
  constructor(name, age, grade) {
    this.name = name;
    this.age = age;
    this.grade = grade;
  }

  displayDetails() {
    console.log(`Student Name: ${this.name}, Age: ${this.age}, Grade:
${this.grade}`);
  }
}

// Creating student objects
const student1 = new Student("Alice", 15, "10th Grade");
const student2 = new Student("Bob", 16, "11th Grade");

// Display details
student1.displayDetails();
student2.displayDetails();
```

Output:

```
Student Name: Alice, Age: 15, Grade: 10th Grade
Student Name: Bob, Age: 16, Grade: 11th Grade
```

Explanation:
- The Student class has **properties** (name, age, grade) and a **method**
  (displayDetails()).
- Two **objects** (student1 and student2) are created and their details
  are displayed.

2. Create a Library System
Solution:

```javascript
class Book {
  constructor(title, author, year) {
    this.title = title;
    this.author = author;
    this.year = year;
  }

  bookInfo() {
    console.log(`"${this.title}" by ${this.author}, published in
${this.year}`);
  }
}

// Creating book objects
const book1 = new Book("The Alchemist", "Paulo Coelho", 1988);
const book2 = new Book("1984", "George Orwell", 1949);

// Display book information
book1.bookInfo();
book2.bookInfo();
```

Output:

```
"The Alchemist" by Paulo Coelho, published in 1988
"1984" by George Orwell, published in 1949
```

Explanation:

- The Book class has **properties** (title, author, year) and a **method** (bookInfo()).
- Two **book objects** (book1 and book2) are created, and their details are displayed.

3. Create an Animal Inheritance System
Solution:

```javascript
// Parent class
class Animal {
  constructor(name) {
    this.name = name;
  }

  makeSound() {
    console.log(`${this.name} makes a sound.`);
```

```
    }
}

// Child class
class Dog extends Animal {
  bark() {
    console.log(`${this.name} barks.`);
  }
}

// Creating a Dog object
const myDog = new Dog("Buddy");

// Calling methods
myDog.makeSound(); // From Animal class
myDog.bark(); // From Dog class
```

Output:

```
Buddy makes a sound.
Buddy barks.
```

Explanation:
- The Animal class is a **parent class** with a makeSound() method.
- The Dog class **inherits** from Animal using extends and has an extra method bark().
- The myDog object calls both methods, demonstrating **inheritance**.

Short Answer Questions and Solutions

1. What is an object in JavaScript?

An **object** is a collection of properties and methods that represent a real-world entity. Objects store data in **key-value pairs**.

Example:

```
let car = { brand: "Toyota", model: "Corolla", year: 2020 };
console.log(car.brand);
```

Output:

```
Toyota
```

2. How do you create a class in JavaScript?

A **class** is created using the class keyword.

Example:

```
class Person {
  constructor(name, age) {
    this.name = name;
    this.age = age;
  }
}
```

3. What is a constructor method used for?

The **constructor** is a special method in a class that initializes **object properties** when a new object is created.

Example:

```
class Person {
  constructor(name, age) {
    this.name = name;
    this.age = age;
  }
}
```

- constructor(name, age) assigns values when an object is created.

4. How do you create an object from a class?

An **object** is created using the new keyword.

Example:

```
const person1 = new Person("John", 30);
```

This creates an instance (person1) of the Person class.

5. What is inheritance in JavaScript?

Inheritance allows a class to **reuse** another class's properties and methods.

Example:

```
class Animal {
  makeSound() {
    console.log("Animal makes a sound.");
  }
}
```

```javascript
class Dog extends Animal {
  bark() {
    console.log("Dog barks.");
  }
}
```

---

6. What does the extends keyword do?

The extends keyword allows a **child class** to inherit from a **parent class**.

Example:

```javascript
class Bird extends Animal {
  fly() {
    console.log("Bird is flying.");
  }
}
```

Here, Bird **inherits** from Animal.

---

7. What is a prototype in JavaScript?

A **prototype** is an object from which other objects inherit properties and methods.

Example:

```javascript
function Person(name) {
  this.name = name;
}
Person.prototype.greet = function () {
  console.log(`Hello, my name is ${this.name}`);
};
```

- Here, greet() is added to the Person prototype.

---

8. How do you add a method to a prototype?

A method can be added to a **prototype** using prototype.methodName.

Example:

```javascript
Person.prototype.sayHi = function () {
  console.log("Hi there!");
};
```

All Person objects can now use sayHi().

---

9. What is the difference between a class and a prototype?

Feature	Classes	Prototypes
Syntax	Uses class keyword	Uses constructor function
Inheritance	Uses extends	Uses prototype chain
Readability	More structured	Less structured

10. Why is OOP useful in JavaScript?

Object-Oriented Programming (OOP) **helps organize** code by:

- **Reusing** properties and methods (Inheritance).
- **Encapsulating** data within objects.
- **Reducing redundancy** by creating reusable structures (Classes).

Example:

```
class Car {
  constructor(brand, model) {
    this.brand = brand;
    this.model = model;
  }
}
```

- This makes creating multiple cars easy.

Summary of Key Concepts

✓ **Objects** store key-value pairs.

✓ **Classes** are blueprints for creating objects.

✓ **Constructor methods** initialize object properties.

✓ **Inheritance** allows reusing properties and methods.

✓ **Prototype** is used for adding shared methods.

✓ **OOP** makes code modular, reusable, and structured.

Assignment Solutions

1. Create a module greet.js that exports a function greet(name), which prints "Hello, name!". Import and use it in another file.

Step 1: Create greet.js (Module File)

```
// greet.js
export function greet(name) {
   console.log(`Hello, ${name}!`);
}
```

Step 2: Create main.js (Import and Use the Function)

```
// main.js
import { greet } from "./greet.js";

greet("Alice");
```

Expected Output:

```
Hello, Alice!
```

Explanation:

- export function greet(name) { ... } exports the greet function.
- import { greet } from "./greet.js"; imports it in main.js.
- Now we can use greet("Alice"), which prints "Hello, Alice!".

2. Create a module math.js that exports functions for multiplication and division. Import them and use them in main.js.

Step 1: Create math.js (Module File)

```
// math.js
export function multiply(a, b) {
   return a * b;
}

export function divide(a, b) {
   if (b === 0) {
      return "Cannot divide by zero!";
   }
   return a / b;
```

```
}
```

Step 2: Create main.js (Import and Use the Functions)

```
// main.js
import { multiply, divide } from "./math.js";

console.log(multiply(5, 3)); // Output: 15
console.log(divide(10, 2));  // Output: 5
console.log(divide(10, 0));  // Output: Cannot divide by zero!
```

Explanation:

- export function multiply(a, b) {...} and export function divide(a, b) {...} export the functions.
- import { multiply, divide } from "./math.js"; imports both functions.
- Now, multiply(5,3) returns 15, and divide(10,2) returns 5.

---

3. Create a module that fetches and displays the title of a post from https://jsonplaceholder.typicode.com/posts/1.

Step 1: Create fetchPost.js (Module File)

```
// fetchPost.js
export async function fetchPostTitle() {
  try {
    let response = await
fetch("https://jsonplaceholder.typicode.com/posts/1");
    let data = await response.json();
    console.log(`Post Title: ${data.title}`);
  } catch (error) {
    console.log("Error fetching post:", error);
  }
}
```

Step 2: Create main.js (Import and Use the Function)

```
// main.js
import { fetchPostTitle } from "./fetchPost.js";

fetchPostTitle();
```

Expected Output (Sample from API):

```
Post Title: sunt aut facere repellat provident occaecati excepturi
optio reprehenderit
```

Explanation:
- fetchPostTitle() fetches the post data using fetch().
- await response.json() extracts JSON data.
- The function logs the **title** of the post.

Short Answer Questions & Explanations

1. What is a module in JavaScript?

A **module** in JavaScript is a file that contains reusable code, such as functions, variables, or classes. Modules help organize and **separate concerns** in large applications.

For example, instead of writing all functions in one file, we can divide them into multiple modules:

```js
// utils.js
export function sayHello() {
   console.log("Hello, World!");
}
// main.js
import { sayHello } from "./utils.js";
sayHello(); // Output: Hello, World!
```

---

2. How do you export a function from a JavaScript module?

To export a function, use the export keyword before defining the function.
Example:

```js
export function greet(name) {
   console.log(`Hello, ${name}!`);
}
```

This allows the function to be imported and used in another file.

---

3. What is the syntax to import a specific function from a module?

Use **named import** syntax:

```js
import { functionName } from "./module.js";
```

Example:

```js
import { greet } from "./greet.js";
greet("Alice");
```

4. Why do we use type="module" in an HTML file?

When using JavaScript **modules**, we must specify <script type="module"> in the HTML file.

Example:

```html
<script type="module" src="main.js"></script>
```

This ensures:

- The script runs in **module mode**.
- import and export statements work correctly.

5. What is the difference between named exports and default exports?

Named Export	Default Export
Exports multiple values.	Exports a single value.
Import using {}.	Import without {}.
Example: export function greet() {}	Example: export default function greet() {}

Example of **named export**:

```js
export function add(a, b) {
   return a + b;
}
Import:
import { add } from "./math.js";
Example of default export:
export default function greet() {
   console.log("Hello!");
}
Import:
import greet from "./greet.js";
```

6. How do you import everything from a module?

Use * to import everything:

```js
import * as math from "./math.js";
console.log(math.multiply(2, 3));
```

Now, functions can be accessed with **math.multiply()**.

7. How do JavaScript modules help in better code organization?

Modules help:

- **Encapsulate code** (reduces conflicts).
- **Reuse functions** across multiple files.
- **Separate concerns** (keep different functionalities in different files).

8. Can you use JavaScript modules in Node.js?

Yes! In Node.js, you can use modules with:

- **CommonJS (require)**
- **ES Modules (import)** (requires "type": "module" in package.json)

Example using CommonJS:

```
const math = require("./math.js");
console.log(math.multiply(2, 3));
Example using ES Modules:
import { multiply } from "./math.js";
console.log(multiply(2, 3));
```

9. What will happen if you forget to use type="module" in an HTML file?

If you don't use type="module", you will get an error:

Uncaught SyntaxError: Cannot use import statement outside a module

Solution: Always use:

```
<script type="module" src="main.js"></script>
```

10. What are the advantages of using JavaScript modules?

1. **Better Code Organization** – Keep related code in separate files.
2. **Reusability** – Write once, use multiple times.
3. **Avoid Global Namespace Pollution** – Each module has its own scope.
4. **Easier Debugging** – Manage code in small, manageable files.
5. **Performance Optimization** – Only import what you need, reducing file size.

Assignment - Practical Exercises

1. Create a simple webpage using Vanilla JavaScript that changes the background color when clicking a button.

Solution:

```html
<!DOCTYPE html>
<html lang="en">
<head>
  <meta charset="UTF-8">
  <meta name="viewport" content="width=device-width, initial-scale=1.0">
  <title>Change Background Color</title>
  <style>
    body {
      text-align: center;
      font-family: Arial, sans-serif;
    }
    button {
      padding: 10px 20px;
      font-size: 18px;
      margin-top: 20px;
      cursor: pointer;
    }
  </style>
</head>
<body>

  <h1>Click the button to change background color</h1>
  <button onclick="changeColor()">Change Color</button>

  <script>
    function changeColor() {
      let colors = ["red", "blue", "green", "yellow", "purple", "orange"];
      let randomColor = colors[Math.floor(Math.random() *
colors.length)];
      document.body.style.backgroundColor = randomColor;
    }
  </script>
```

```
</body>
</html>
```

Explanation:
- We create a simple HTML page with a button.
- When the button is clicked, JavaScript picks a random color from an array.
- The background color changes dynamically.

---

2. Build a basic React component that displays "Hello, [Your Name]" dynamically.
Solution:

```jsx
import React, { useState } from "react";

function Greeting() {
  const [name, setName] = useState("");

  return (
    <div style={{ textAlign: "center", marginTop: "50px" }}>
      <h2>Hello, {name ? name : "Guest"}!</h2>
      <input
        type="text"
        placeholder="Enter your name"
        onChange={(e) => setName(e.target.value)}
      />
    </div>
  );
}

export default Greeting;
```

Explanation:
- We use **React useState hook** to store user input.
- If no name is entered, it shows "Hello, Guest!" by default.
- When the user types their name, it updates dynamically.

---

3. Make a simple Vue.js app that takes user input and displays it on the screen.
Solution:

```html
<!DOCTYPE html>
<html lang="en">
```

```html
<head>
  <meta charset="UTF-8">
  <meta name="viewport" content="width=device-width, initial-scale=1.0">
  <title>Vue.js Input Example</title>
  <script src="https://cdn.jsdelivr.net/npm/vue@2.6.14/dist/vue.js"></script>
</head>
<body>

  <div id="app">
    <h2>Hello, {{ name }}</h2>
    <input type="text" v-model="name" placeholder="Enter your name">
  </div>

  <script>
    new Vue({
      el: "#app",
      data: {
        name: "Guest"
      }
    });
  </script>

</body>
</html>
```

Explanation:

- **Vue.js uses two-way data binding** (v-model) to update the name dynamically.
- When the user types, the text updates automatically.
- Default text is **"Hello, Guest"**.

Short Answer Questions and Solutions

1. What is a JavaScript framework?

A **JavaScript framework** is a **pre-written collection of JavaScript code** that helps developers build applications faster. It provides **structured code, reusable components, and built-in functions** to handle common tasks like UI updates, data management, and routing.

Example: **React, Vue.js, Angular**.

2. Name three popular JavaScript frameworks.

1. **React.js** – Developed by Facebook, used for building user interfaces.
2. **Vue.js** – A progressive framework, easy to learn, used for web applications.
3. **Angular.js** – Developed by Google, a full-fledged framework for web apps.

3. How does React differ from Vue.js?

Feature	React	Vue.js
Developed By	Facebook	Evan You (Community-driven)
Type	Library	Framework
Learning Curve	Medium	Easy
Data Binding	One-way	Two-way
Speed	Fast	Lightweight and Fast
Use Case	Large apps	Small to medium apps

React focuses on **component-based architecture**, while Vue is easier for beginners due to its **simpler syntax**.

4. What is a component in React?

A **component** is a **reusable piece of UI** that contains its own structure, style, and behavior.

Example of a React functional component:

```
function Hello() {
   return <h1>Hello, World!</h1>;
}
```

5. Why is Vue.js considered beginner-friendly?

- **Easy to learn** – Uses simple HTML, CSS, and JavaScript.
- **Two-way data binding** – Automatically updates UI when data changes.
- **Lightweight** – Smaller in size compared to React and Angular.

Example:

```
<input v-model="message">
<p>{{ message }}</p>
```

This automatically updates text as the user types.

---

6. What company developed Angular?

Google developed Angular. It is a **TypeScript-based** front-end framework for building web applications.

---

7. When should you use Vanilla JavaScript instead of a framework?

- When building **small or simple projects** like **landing pages**.
- When **performance is critical** (no extra dependencies).
- When learning **core JavaScript concepts** before moving to frameworks.

Example:

```
document.getElementById("btn").addEventListener("click", function()
{
   alert("Hello from Vanilla JavaScript!");
});
```

---

8. What does two-way data binding mean in Vue.js?

Two-way data binding means that **changes in the UI automatically update the data, and vice versa**.

Example:

```
<input v-model="name">
<p>{{ name }}</p>
```

When a user types in the input field, the paragraph updates automatically.

---

9. What is the main advantage of using a JavaScript framework?

- **Faster Development** – Pre-built features reduce coding time.
- **Reusable Components** – Save time by reusing UI elements.
- **Better Performance** – Optimized for efficiency.
- **Easier Maintenance** – Structured code helps in debugging and updates.

Example:

```
// React Component
function Greeting({ name }) {
   return <h1>Hello, {name}!</h1>;
}
```

This component can be **reused** multiple times with different names.

---

10. What does "SPA" stand for in web development?
SPA stands for Single-Page Application.

- It **loads only one HTML page** and updates content dynamically **without reloading the entire page**.
- Example: **Gmail, Facebook, Twitter**.

Example using Vue.js:

```
<div id="app">
  <router-view></router-view> <!-- Loads components dynamically --
>
</div>
```

Summary of Key Takeaways

- **JavaScript frameworks** help build web apps faster and more efficiently.
- **React, Vue.js, and Angular** are the most popular frameworks.
- **Vue.js is easy for beginners**, while **React is great for large-scale applications**.
- **Two-way data binding** in Vue.js makes UI updates automatic.
- **JavaScript frameworks help build SPAs (Single-Page Applications)**.

Assignment Solutions

1. Modify the web app to display a "Good Morning" or "Good Evening" message based on the current time.

Solution:

We use JavaScript's Date object to check the current hour and display a message accordingly.

```
<!DOCTYPE html>
<html lang="en">
<head>
  <title>Greeting Message</title>
</head>
<body>
  <h2 id="greeting"></h2>

  <script>
    function displayGreeting() {
      let now = new Date();
      let hour = now.getHours();
      let message = (hour < 12) ? "Good Morning!" : "Good Evening!";
      document.getElementById("greeting").innerText = message;
    }

    displayGreeting();
  </script>
</body>
</html>
```

Output (if time is 10 AM):

Good Morning!

Output (if time is 7 PM):

Good Evening!

2. Add a reset button to clear the input field and reset the displayed message.

Solution:
We use an input field and a button to reset the content.

```html
<!DOCTYPE html>
<html lang="en">
<head>
  <title>Reset Input</title>
</head>
<body>
  <input type="text" id="userInput" placeholder="Type something here">
  <p id="message">Hello!</p>
  <button onclick="resetFields()">Reset</button>

  <script>
    function resetFields() {
        document.getElementById("userInput").value = "";
        document.getElementById("message").innerText = "Hello!";
    }
  </script>
</body>
</html>
```

Explanation:

- Clicking the **Reset** button clears the input field and resets the message.

---

3. Create a counter that starts at 10 and decreases each time a button is clicked.

Solution:

We create a counter and update it every time the button is clicked.

```html
<!DOCTYPE html>
<html lang="en">
<head>
  <title>Countdown</title>
</head>
<body>
  <h2>Counter: <span id="counter">10</span></h2>
  <button onclick="decreaseCounter()">Decrease</button>

  <script>
    let count = 10;
```

```
    function decreaseCounter() {
      if (count > 0) {
        count--;
        document.getElementById("counter").innerText = count;
      }
    }
  </script>
</body>
</html>
```

Explanation:

- Clicking the **Decrease** button reduces the counter value by 1.

Short Answer Questions and Explanations

1. What are the three main technologies used in web development?

The three core technologies for web development are:

1. **HTML (HyperText Markup Language)** – Defines the structure of a webpage.
2. **CSS (Cascading Style Sheets)** – Styles the webpage (colors, fonts, layouts).
3. **JavaScript** – Adds interactivity and dynamic behavior.

---

2. What is the purpose of JavaScript in a web page?

JavaScript is used to:

- Make web pages interactive.
- Handle user inputs.
- Update content dynamically (e.g., real-time clocks, form validation).
- Communicate with servers using AJAX and APIs.

Example:

```
document.getElementById("demo").innerText = "Hello, World!";
```

---

3. How do you create a button in HTML?

A button is created using the <button> tag.
Example:

```
<button>Click Me</button>
A button that triggers JavaScript:
<button onclick="alert('Hello!')">Click Me</button>
```

4. What does document.getElementById() do?

It selects an HTML element by its id.
Example:

```
document.getElementById("demo").innerText = "New Text!";
```

5. How can you change the text color dynamically using JavaScript?

Using the style.color property.
Example:

```
document.getElementById("text").style.color = "blue";
```

6. What is an event in JavaScript?

An event is an action that happens in the browser, like clicking, hovering, or typing.
Example of a **click event**:

```
document.getElementById("btn").addEventListener("click", function()
{
   alert("Button Clicked!");
});
```

7. How do you write a function in JavaScript?

A function is declared using the function keyword.
Example:

```
function sayHello() {
   console.log("Hello, World!");
}
sayHello();
```

8. What does setInterval() do?

It repeatedly executes a function after a fixed time interval.
Example:

```
setInterval(() => console.log("Hello every 2 seconds"), 2000);
```

This prints **"Hello every 2 seconds"** indefinitely.

9. How do you link an external CSS file to an HTML file?

Use the <link> tag inside <head>.
Example:

```
<link rel="stylesheet" href="styles.css">
```

This links the **styles.css** file to the HTML page.

---

10. What happens when you use innerHTML in JavaScript?

The innerHTML property changes the content inside an element.
Example:

```
document.getElementById("demo").innerHTML = "<b>Bold
Text</b>";
```

Output:
The text inside demo becomes bold.

Summary of Key Concepts

- **JavaScript makes web pages interactive** (e.g., button clicks, animations).
- **Events** trigger actions based on user input (e.g., onclick).
- **DOM Manipulation** allows JavaScript to modify HTML elements (innerText, innerHTML).
- **CSS Styling with JavaScript** changes styles dynamically (style.color).
- **setInterval()** executes a function repeatedly.

Assignment Solutions
Exercise 1: Fix the Formatting
Given Code:

```
function calc(a,b){return a+b;}
console.log(calc(5,10));
```

Formatted Code (Readable and Cleaned-up Version):

```
function calc(a, b) {
    return a + b;
}


console.log(calc(5, 10));
```

Changes Made:
- Added proper indentation and spacing for better readability.
- Used line breaks to separate function declaration and execution.

Exercise 2: Optimize the Loop
Given Code (Using a for Loop):

```
let colors = ["Red", "Blue", "Green"];
for (let i = 0; i < colors.length; i++) {
    console.log(colors[i]);
}
```

Optimized Code (Using .forEach()):

```
let colors = ["Red", "Blue", "Green"];
colors.forEach(color => console.log(color));
```

Why is .forEach() better?
- Reduces the need for an index variable (i).
- Improves code readability.
- Uses a built-in array method specifically designed for iteration.

Exercise 3: Secure the Input
Given Code (Without Validation):

```
let userAge = prompt("Enter your age:");
```

```javascript
console.log("Your age is: " + userAge);
```

Fixed Code (With Validation to Allow Only Numbers):

```javascript
let userAge = prompt("Enter your age:");

if (!isNaN(userAge) && userAge.trim() !== "") {
  console.log("Your age is: " + userAge);
} else {
  console.log("Invalid input! Please enter a valid number.");
}
```

Changes Made:

- **isNaN(userAge)** ensures that only numbers are accepted.
- **trim()** removes spaces to prevent empty input.
- **Error message** for invalid input.

Short Answer Questions and Explanations

1. Why is using meaningful variable names important?

- Makes code easier to **read and understand**.
- Helps developers **collaborate** efficiently.
- Reduces the chances of **confusion and errors**.

Example (Bad Naming):

```javascript
let x = 5;
let y = 10;
let z = x + y;
console.log(z);
```

Example (Good Naming):

```javascript
let num1 = 5;
let num2 = 10;
let sum = num1 + num2;
console.log(sum);
```

2. What is the DRY principle?

DRY (Don't Repeat Yourself) means **avoiding code repetition** by using functions, loops, or modules.

Example (Without DRY – Repetitive Code):

```javascript
console.log("Hello, John!");
```

```
console.log("Hello, Jane!");
console.log("Hello, Mike!");
```

Example (With DRY – Using a Function):

```
function greet(name) {
    console.log("Hello, " + name + "!");
}


greet("John");
greet("Jane");
greet("Mike");
```

Benefit: Reduces redundancy, makes maintenance easier.

3. Why should you avoid eval()?

- **Security Risk:** It allows execution of malicious code.
- **Performance Issue:** Slows down the application.
- **Hard to Debug:** Makes debugging complex.

Bad Example (Using eval())

```
let userInput = "2 + 2";
console.log(eval(userInput)); // Potential security risk
```

Better Alternative (Without eval())

```
let userInput = "2 + 2";
console.log(Function('"use strict"; return (' + userInput + ')')());
```

4. What is the difference between var, let, and const?

Keyword	Scope	Reassignment	Redeclaration	Hoisting
var	Function	Yes	Yes	Hoisted with undefined
let	Block	Yes	✖ No	Hoisted but not initialized
const	Block	✖ No	✖ No	Hoisted but not initialized

Example:

```
var x = 10;  // Can be redeclared
let y = 20;  // Cannot be redeclared
const z = 30; // Cannot be changed
```

5. Why is input validation necessary?

- **Prevents incorrect data entry.**
- **Reduces security vulnerabilities.**
- **Improves user experience.**

Example (Without Validation – Problematic):

```
let age = prompt("Enter your age:");
console.log("You entered: " + age);
```

Example (With Validation – Secure):

```
let age = prompt("Enter your age:");
if (!isNaN(age) && age.trim() !== "") {
   console.log("Your age is: " + age);
} else {
   console.log("Invalid input! Please enter a valid number.");
}
```

6. What is the benefit of using .forEach()?

- **Simplifies looping through arrays.**
- **Removes the need for an index variable.**
- **More readable and efficient.**

Example:

```
let numbers = [10, 20, 30];
numbers.forEach(num => console.log(num));
```

7. Why should functions be small and focused?

- Easier to **debug and test**.
- Promotes **code reusability**.
- Improves **readability**.

Example (Bad – Too Long Function):

```
function processNumbers(numbers) {
   let sum = 0;
   for (let num of numbers) {
      sum += num;
   }
   let avg = sum / numbers.length;
   console.log("Sum:", sum);
   console.log("Average:", avg);
}
```

Example (Good – Small, Focused Functions):

```javascript
function calculateSum(numbers) {
   return numbers.reduce((total, num) => total + num, 0);
}

function calculateAverage(numbers) {
   return calculateSum(numbers) / numbers.length;
}
```

---

8. How does asynchronous JavaScript improve performance?

- **Prevents blocking the main thread.**
- **Allows multiple tasks to run simultaneously.**
- **Improves user experience with fast UI interactions.**

Example (Asynchronous Fetch API):

```javascript
fetch('https://api.example.com/data')
   .then(response => response.json())
   .then(data => console.log(data));
```

---

9. What is a security risk of using var?

- **var is function-scoped**, meaning it **can be accessed outside of loops or blocks**, leading to unintended behavior.

Example (Problem with var):

```javascript
if (true) {
   var x = 10;
}
console.log(x); // No error! But should be block-scoped.
```

Solution (Use let or const instead):

```javascript
if (true) {
   let x = 10;
}
console.log(x); // Error! x is not defined.
```

---

10. How does async/await help in handling API requests?

- **Makes asynchronous code look synchronous.**
- **Reduces callback hell.**
- **Easier to debug and maintain.**

Example (Using async/await for API calls):

```
async function fetchData() {
   let response = await
fetch("https://jsonplaceholder.typicode.com/posts/1");
   let data = await response.json();
   console.log(data);
}
fetchData();
```

Summary of key Concepts

- **Use meaningful variable names.**
- **Follow the DRY principle.**
- **Avoid eval() for security.**
- **Use let and const instead of var.**
- **Always validate user input.**
- **Use .forEach() for cleaner loops.**
- **Write small, focused functions.**
- **Use async/await for cleaner asynchronous code.**

Assignment Solutions

1. Write a Node.js program that creates a new file and writes "Learning Node.js is fun!" into it.

Solution:

We use the fs (File System) module in Node.js to create and write to a file.

```
const fs = require('fs');

fs.writeFile("node_example.txt", "Learning Node.js is fun!", (err) => {
   if (err) {
      console.error("Error writing file:", err);
   } else {
      console.log("File created and content written successfully!");
   }
});
```

Output:

```
File created and content written successfully!
```

2. Modify the previous program to read the content of the file and display it in the console.

Solution:

We use fs.readFile() to read the content of the file.

```
const fs = require('fs');

fs.readFile("node_example.txt", "utf8", (err, data) => {
   if (err) {
      console.error("Error reading file:", err);
   } else {
      console.log("File Content:", data);
   }
});
```

Output:

```
File Content: Learning Node.js is fun!
```

3. Create a basic Node.js web server that responds with "Welcome to my website!" when visited.

Solution:

We use the built-in http module to create a simple server.

```
const http = require('http');

const server = http.createServer((req, res) => {
  res.writeHead(200, { "Content-Type": "text/plain" });
  res.end("Welcome to my website!");
});

server.listen(3000, () => {
  console.log("Server running at http://localhost:3000");
});
```

How to Run:

- Save the file as server.js
- Run: node server.js
- Open a browser and visit http://localhost:3000
- You will see **"Welcome to my website!"**

Short Answer Questions and Solutions

1. What is Node.js?

Answer:

Node.js is a **runtime environment** that allows JavaScript to be executed **outside the browser**. It is built on Chrome's V8 engine and is mainly used for **server-side applications**.

---

2. Why is Node.js useful for web development?

Answer:

Node.js is useful because:

- It is **fast and scalable** due to its **non-blocking** event-driven architecture.
- It allows **full-stack development** using JavaScript (both frontend and backend).
- It has a large ecosystem with **npm (Node Package Manager)** for easy package management.

---

3. How do you install Node.js on your computer?

Answer:

- Download Node.js from nodejs.org and install it.

- Check if the installation was successful using:
- node -v

---

4. How can you check the installed Node.js version?
Answer:
Use the following command in the terminal or command prompt:
node -v
Example Output:
v18.14.0

---

5. What command is used to run a JavaScript file in Node.js?
Answer:
The command to run a JavaScript file in Node.js is:
node filename.js
Example:
node server.js

---

6. What is the http module used for?
Answer:
The http module in Node.js is used to create an **HTTP server** that can handle client requests and send responses.
Example:

```
const http = require('http');
```

---

7. Write a simple command to create a file using Node.js.
Answer:
Using the fs.writeFile() method:

```
const fs = require('fs');

fs.writeFile("example.txt", "Hello, Node.js!", (err) => {
  if (err) throw err;
  console.log("File created successfully!");
});
```

---

8. How do you delete a file using Node.js?
Answer:
Use fs.unlink() to delete a file.
Example:

```
const fs = require('fs');

fs.unlink("example.txt", (err) => {
  if (err) throw err;
  console.log("File deleted successfully!");
});
```

9. What does fs.readFile() do?
Answer:
fs.readFile() reads the content of a file asynchronously.
Example:

```
const fs = require('fs');

fs.readFile("example.txt", "utf8", (err, data) => {
  if (err) throw err;
  console.log(data);
});
```

10. Mention two real-world use cases of Node.js.
Answer:
1. **Building APIs and Microservices** – Companies like Netflix use Node.js for fast and scalable backend services.
2. **Real-time Applications** – Used in **chat applications, online gaming, and collaborative tools** like Slack.

Summary of Key Concepts

- **Node.js** is a JavaScript runtime for server-side development.
- **fs module** handles file operations like read, write, and delete.
- **http module** is used to create web servers.
- **Run a Node.js file** using node filename.js.
- **Install Node.js** from nodejs.org.

This section provides solutions for the **Hour 24 Assignment** and **Short Answer Questions** to finalize the JavaScript To-Do App with additional functionalities.

❖ Assignment Solutions

1. Modify the app to edit a task when double-clicked.

We can allow users to edit a task by listening for a **double-click** event on a list item (li). When double-clicked, the task should become an input field so users can update it.

Solution:

```javascript
document.querySelector("#taskList").addEventListener("dblclick",
function(event) {
  if (event.target.tagName === "LI") {
    let currentText = event.target.innerText;
    let input = document.createElement("input");
    input.type = "text";
    input.value = currentText;

    // Replace the task text with an input field
    event.target.innerHTML = "";
    event.target.appendChild(input);
    input.focus();

    // Save the new task when the user presses Enter
    input.addEventListener("keypress", function(e) {
      if (e.key === "Enter" && input.value.trim() !== "") {
        event.target.innerText = input.value;
      }
    });

    // If user clicks outside, restore the text
    input.addEventListener("blur", function() {
      event.target.innerText = input.value || currentText;
    });
  }
});
```

2. Add a "Clear All" button to remove all tasks at once.

A **"Clear All"** button allows users to remove all tasks from the list.
Solution:

```javascript
document.querySelector("#clearAllBtn").addEventListener("click",
function() {
    document.querySelector("#taskList").innerHTML = "";
    localStorage.removeItem("tasks"); // Remove from Local Storage
});
```

Adding the Button in HTML

```html
<button id="clearAllBtn">Clear All</button>
```

3. Customize the app by adding colors, fonts, or animations.

We can enhance the UI by applying styles with CSS.

Solution: (CSS Customization)

```css
body {
    font-family: Arial, sans-serif;
    background-color: #f8f9fa;
}

li {
    background: #ffffff;
    color: #333;
    padding: 10px;
    margin: 5px 0;
    border-radius: 5px;
    transition: background 0.3s;
}

li:hover {
    background: #f1f1f1;
    cursor: pointer;
}

button {
    background-color: #007bff;
    color: white;
    padding: 8px 12px;
    border: none;
    cursor: pointer;
    transition: 0.3s;
```

```css
}

button:hover {
  background-color: #0056b3;
}
```

- **Added smooth transitions** for list items and buttons.
- **Styled fonts and backgrounds** to make the UI visually appealing.

Short Answer Questions and Solutions

1. What is Local Storage in JavaScript?

Local Storage is a browser feature that allows storing data **persistently** across sessions. The data is stored as key-value pairs and does not expire until manually cleared.

Example:

```javascript
localStorage.setItem("name", "John"); // Save data
console.log(localStorage.getItem("name")); // Retrieve data
localStorage.removeItem("name"); // Remove data
```

2. How does addEventListener() work?

The addEventListener() method attaches an event handler to an element.

Example:

```javascript
document.querySelector("#btn").addEventListener("click", function()
{
  console.log("Button Clicked!");
});
```

- It allows multiple event handlers to be attached to the same element.

3. What is the difference between .classList.add() and .classList.toggle()?

Method	Description
.classList.add("className")	Adds a class to an element
.classList.toggle("className")	Adds the class if it's missing; removes it if it's already there

Example:

```
document.querySelector("#box").classList.add("highlight");
document.querySelector("#box").classList.toggle("hidden"); // Adds
or removes "hidden" class
```

---

4. How does JSON.stringify() help in saving data?

JSON.stringify() converts JavaScript objects into a string format suitable for storage.

Example:

```
let tasks = ["Task 1", "Task 2"];
localStorage.setItem("tasks", JSON.stringify(tasks)); // Save
let savedTasks = JSON.parse(localStorage.getItem("tasks")); //
Retrieve
console.log(savedTasks); // ["Task 1", "Task 2"]
```

---

5. Why do we use DOMContentLoaded in JavaScript?

DOMContentLoaded ensures JavaScript runs **after** the HTML has loaded.

Example:

```
document.addEventListener("DOMContentLoaded", function() {
    console.log("DOM fully loaded!");
});
```

- This prevents JavaScript from running before elements exist.

---

6. What happens when you call taskList.removeChild(li)?

It removes the **specified child element** (li) from the taskList.

Example:

```
let taskList = document.querySelector("#taskList");
let taskItem = document.querySelector("li");
taskList.removeChild(taskItem);
```

- If the li exists, it will be removed from the list.

---

7. What does querySelectorAll() do?

querySelectorAll() selects **all matching elements** and returns a **NodeList**.

Example:

```
let items = document.querySelectorAll("li");
console.log(items.length); // Outputs the number of <li> elements
```

---

8. How can you prevent an empty task from being added?
Before adding a task, check if the input is empty.
Example:

```javascript
document.querySelector("#addBtn").addEventListener("click",
function() {
    let taskInput = document.querySelector("#taskInput").value.trim();
    if (taskInput === "") {
        alert("Task cannot be empty!");
    } else {
        // Add task to the list
    }
});
```

9. What are the advantages of using JavaScript for front-end development?

✔ **Interactivity:** Enables dynamic changes (e.g., animations, pop-ups).

✔ **Fast Execution:** Runs in the browser without server requests.

✔ **Rich Ecosystem:** Many libraries (React, Vue, jQuery) for enhancing UI.

✔ **Works Across Platforms:** Runs on all browsers without extra installations.

10. How can you enhance this To-Do app further?
Add more features like:

✔ **Task due dates** (allow users to set deadlines).

✔ **Priority levels** (high, medium, low).

✔ **Drag and drop tasks** for better organization.

✔ **Dark mode toggle** for better UI customization.

✔ **Sync with cloud storage** to access tasks from any device.

Final Thoughts
This wraps up **Hour 24: JavaScript To-Do App Enhancements**! You now have a **fully functional** To-Do App with **editing, clearing, and customization options**.

A.1 Assignment Solutions

1. Write a JavaScript program that displays "Welcome to JavaScript Learning!" inside a webpage.

Solution:

To display text inside a webpage, we can use document.write() or manipulate the HTML using JavaScript.

```html
<!DOCTYPE html>
<html lang="en">
<head>
  <title>JavaScript Welcome Message</title>
</head>
<body>
  <script>
    document.write("Welcome to JavaScript Learning!");
  </script>
</body>
</html>
```

Output:

It will display **"Welcome to JavaScript Learning!"** on the webpage.

2. Declare three variables (name, age, city) and print them using console.log().

Solution:

```javascript
let name = "John";
let age = 25;
let city = "New York";

console.log("Name:", name);
console.log("Age:", age);
console.log("City:", city);
```

Output:

```
Name: John
Age: 25
City: New York
```

Explanation:

- let is used to declare variables.
- console.log() is used to print values to the browser console.

---

3. Perform a simple calculation: Add 25 and 10, and display the result.
Solution:

```
let result = 25 + 10;
console.log("The sum is:", result);
```

Output:

```
The sum is: 35
```

Explanation:

- The + operator adds two numbers.
- The result is stored in the result variable and displayed using console.log().

Short Answer Questions and Solutions

1. What is JavaScript?
Answer:

JavaScript is a **programming language** used to create **interactive and dynamic** web pages. It allows developers to add functionality such as animations, form validation, and user interactions.

Example:

```
alert("Hello, this is JavaScript!");
```

---

2. How does JavaScript make web pages interactive?
Answer:

JavaScript interacts with HTML and CSS to add functionality like:

- **Validating forms** (checking if fields are filled)
- **Creating animations**
- **Handling events** (like button clicks)
- **Fetching and displaying data dynamically**

Example:

```
document.getElementById("myButton").onclick = function() {
    alert("Button clicked!");
};
```

3. What are the three ways to write JavaScript?

Answer:

1. **Inline JavaScript** (inside an HTML element)

```
<button onclick="alert('Hello!')">Click me</button>
```

2. **Internal JavaScript** (inside a <script> tag in HTML)

```
<script>
  alert("Hello from internal JavaScript!");
</script>
```

3. **External JavaScript** (linked via a separate .js file)

```
<script src="script.js"></script>
```

---

4. What is the difference between var, let, and const?

Keyword	Scope	Reassignment	Redeclaration	Hoisting
var	Function-scoped	Yes	Yes	Hoisted with undefined
let	Block-scoped	Yes	No	Hoisted but not initialized
const	Block-scoped	No	No	Hoisted but not initialized

Example:

```
var x = 10;
let y = 20;
const z = 30;
```

---

5. Why is JavaScript case-sensitive?

Answer:

JavaScript is case-sensitive because:

- var name and var Name are different variables.
- It ensures proper distinction between methods (toUpperCase() vs touppercase()).

Example:

```
let Name = "Alice";
let name = "Bob";
console.log(Name); // Alice
```

```
console.log(name); // Bob
```

6. What is an operator in JavaScript?

Answer:

An **operator** is a symbol used to perform operations on variables.

- **Arithmetic operators** (+, -, *, /)
- **Comparison operators** (==, !=, >, <)
- **Logical operators** (&&, ||, !)

Example:

```
let sum = 10 + 5;
console.log(sum); // 15
```

7. How do you store values in JavaScript?

Answer:

Values are stored in **variables** using var, let, or const.

Example:

```
let age = 25;
let city = "New York";
console.log(age, city);
```

Output:

```
25 New York
```

8. What is the purpose of semicolons in JavaScript?

Answer:

Semicolons **separate statements** and **prevent errors** in JavaScript.

Example:

```
let a = 10;
let b = 20;
console.log(a + b);
```

Even though JavaScript can sometimes omit semicolons, it is good practice to use them.

9. Write a simple JavaScript program that multiplies two numbers.

Answer:

```
let num1 = 5;
```

```
let num2 = 4;
let result = num1 * num2;
console.log("Multiplication Result:", result);
```

Output:

```
Multiplication Result: 20
```

10. What is an example of a real-life use case for JavaScript?

Answer:

JavaScript is used in **real-world applications** such as:

- **Web development** (interactive forms, dynamic pages)
- **Gaming** (browser-based games)
- **Mobile apps** (React Native for mobile development)
- **Data visualization** (charts and graphs)

Example:

```
document.getElementById("demo").innerHTML = "JavaScript is awesome!";
```
This modifies the content of a webpage dynamically.

Summary of Key Concepts

- **JavaScript is a scripting language for web interactivity.**
- **There are three ways to write JavaScript: Inline, Internal, and External.**
- **Operators perform actions on variables.**
- **Semicolons (;) separate statements.**
- **var, let, and const have different scopes and behaviors.**
- **Real-world JavaScript use cases include web development, gaming, and data visualization.**

Assignment Solutions – Fixing Errors in JavaScript

In JavaScript, errors can occur due to incorrect syntax, missing elements, or logical mistakes. Let's go through the practical exercises and short-answer questions one by one.

Practical Exercises – Fixing Errors in JavaScript

1. Fix the following code to display "Hello, John" in the console:

Given Code (Incorrect)

```
let name = "John"
console.log(Hello, name);
```

Fixed Code:

```
let name = "John";
console.log("Hello, " + name);
```

Output:

```
Hello, John
```

Mistakes Fixed:

- Hello was not inside quotes, causing a **ReferenceError.**
- The string "Hello, " was enclosed in **double quotes**.
- **Semicolon (;) added** at the end of the first line (best practice).

2. Correct the missing function syntax in the code below:

Given Code (Incorrect)

```
function greet
} console.log("Hello!");
greet();
```

Fixed Code:

```
function greet() {
    console.log("Hello!");
}
greet();
```

Output:

```
Hello!
```

Mistakes Fixed:

- function greet was missing parentheses ().
- The **opening curly brace {** was missing after function greet().
- The function **wasn't defined properly** before calling greet();.

---

3. Identify and fix the error in this code:
Given Code (Incorrect)

```
let number = 10;
if number > 5 {
    console.log("Big number!");
}
```

Fixed Code:

```
let number = 10;
if (number > 5) {
    console.log("Big number!");
}
```

Output:

```
Big number!
```

Mistakes Fixed:

- The **if condition** was missing parentheses () around the condition.
- if number > 5 was corrected to if (number > 5).

Short Answer Questions & Solutions

1. What is a JavaScript error?
A **JavaScript error** occurs when the JavaScript engine encounters something it cannot execute, such as **incorrect syntax, missing variables, or calling undefined functions**.
Example:

```
console.log(Hello); // ReferenceError: Hello is not defined
```

Solution: Use **quotes** around "Hello".

---

2. What causes a SyntaxError?
A **SyntaxError** occurs when JavaScript code is written incorrectly and doesn't follow the proper rules.
Example:

```
console.log("Hello" // Missing closing parenthesis
```

Solution: Always ensure brackets (), {}, "" are properly closed.

3. How do you fix a ReferenceError?

A **ReferenceError** occurs when trying to use a variable or function that hasn't been declared.

Example:

```
console.log(myName); // ReferenceError: myName is not defined
```

Fix: Declare the variable before using it.

```
let myName = "Alice";
console.log(myName);
```

4. What is a TypeError in JavaScript?

A **TypeError** occurs when an operation is performed on a value of the wrong type.

Example:

```
let num = 10;
console.log(num.toUpperCase()); // TypeError: num.toUpperCase is
not a function
```

Fix: Use the correct method for the data type.

5. Why does console.log(Hello World); give an error?

The **error** occurs because "Hello World" is not inside quotes.

Incorrect:

```
console.log(Hello World);
```

Fixed Code:

```
console.log("Hello World");
```

6. What should always be wrapped in quotes in JavaScript?

Strings must always be wrapped in **single (') or double (") quotes**.

Example:

```
let greeting = "Hello!";
console.log(greeting); // Correct
console.log(Hello!); // Error
```

7. How can you debug errors in JavaScript?

JavaScript errors can be **debugged** using:

1. console.log() – Print values to the console.
2. **Browser Developer Tools** (F12 → Console tab).
3. **Debugger keyword** – Stops execution for debugging.
4. **Linting tools** like ESLint to catch errors early.

Example:

```
let x = 5;
debugger; // Execution stops here for debugging
console.log(x);
```

8. What happens if you try to call a number as a function?

If you try to call a **number** as a function, it results in a **TypeError**.
Example:

```
let num = 5;
num(); // TypeError: num is not a function
```

Fix: Only call functions using ().

9. Why is it important to declare variables before using them?

Variables **must** be declared before using them, otherwise, a **ReferenceError** occurs.
Example:

```
console.log(myVar); // ReferenceError
let myVar = 10;
```

Fix: Declare let myVar = 10; before console.log().

10. What is the best way to prevent JavaScript errors?

✔ Use **strict mode**:

```
"use strict";
x = 10; // ✖ Error: x is not defined
```

✔ Always check for **missing syntax** (like brackets {}, quotes "").

✔ Use console.log() to check values before using them.

✔ Keep functions **well-defined** before calling them.

- **Syntax Errors** happen when JavaScript code is **incorrectly written**.
- **ReferenceErrors** occur when trying to use a **variable that isn't declared**.
- **TypeErrors** happen when trying to use the wrong type of value in an operation.
- **Debugging** is done using console.log(), browser dev tools, and the debugger statement.
- **Using strict mode ("use strict")** prevents accidental errors.

Notes

Notes

Notes